CONTENTS

ON BILL

BY KARIN GIMMI

THE FATAL SUCCESS OF 'CONCRETE ART'

It must have been sometime in the mid-1990s, during
a period of intense engagement with Max Bill at the
University of Zurich, that a student brought me a bilious
green poster with black lettering – a kind of handbill
or flyer that he'd found stuck on the wall of a house
somewhere in the city. Written on it, in capital letters,
was the following declaration:

> ROLF KNIE AND MAX BILL
>
> ARE NOT THE MOST IMPORTANT
>
> SWISS ARTISTS

Readers unacquainted with the local Zurich scene at that
time should know that Rolf Knie was a scion of a Swiss
circus dynasty whose career trajectory had taken him from
clown to performing artiste to the fine arts. In the 1990s
Knie was not only attracting attention with his subjects
from the circus world but was also busy experimenting
with acid etching on canvas, painting on circus tent fabric
and designing animal costumes for Disneyworld in Florida.
Knie ranked as a successful artist, with the public as well
as commercially, and he was often profiled in the tabloid
press. It is not possible to establish for certain the prov-
enance of the above-mentioned green poster. Given its
provocative, ironic content and its ad-hoc composition, it
should perhaps be seen in the context of those 1980s/90s

(street-)art movements in Zurich that used graffiti, illegally daubed Sponti slogans and anonymous placards to turn public space into a stage for cultural action and performance. Or perhaps the whole thing was just some art history students' idea of a joke. In any case, while textually not very inspired, the words communicated a message that was quite unequivocal and clearly symptomatic of a certain state of mind at the time.

Max Bill, born in 1908 in Winterthur, an industrial town near Zurich, was at the time of his death in 1994 a star on the international art scene. Yet younger artists in Switzerland not only had begun to question Bill's modernism, but also now saw the former avant-garde artist as part of an establishment that had wholeheartedly embraced the socio-political status quo. This was the very same Bill who, on being awarded the 'Art Prize of the City of Zurich' in 1968, had titled his acceptance speech 'Das Behagen im Kleinstaat' (meaning roughly 'small-town contentment'). Hence the Bentley, which Bill drove with a discernible sense of pride, was no longer discussed only in terms of its 'good design' but as a status symbol that was simply inappropriate for an artist who wished to be taken seriously.[1] Like Knie, albeit on a totally different stylistic and artistic level, Bill had (at least according to his critics) sold out and translated his art into a slick commercial formula.

These reservations about Bill and his art did not just stem from the typical resentments and jealousies of local politics. More fundamentally, they reflected a sense that there was an axis of success that ran directly from the proponents of a politically unimpeachable neutral, abstract or concrete art to the representatives of the capitalist system.[2] The monumental marble sculptures that large banking institutions commissioned from Max Bill in the 1980s seem to lend weight to this perception. Thus, for example, the *Pavilion Sculpture* of 1983, financed by the Schweizerische Bankgesellschaft (now the UBS) and gifted to the city of Zurich, tellingly (and despite protests from the man in the street) found a home on Zurich's Bahnhof-

Max Bill as organiser of the Swiss Werkbund's exhibition at the Museum
of Applied Arts in Zurich, 1940. © HDK, Hochschule der Künste, Zurich

strasse, the epicentre of the city's luxury shopping, business and banking system. Three years later, the Deutsche Bank chose a version of Bill's sculpture *Continuity*, executed in polished marble of pharaonic dimensions, to adorn its Frankfurt headquarters. The alliance between Bill and the banks now appeared to be literally set in stone.[3]

By the mid-1990s, the critical reception of the ideology and impact of Concrete Art had reached its (provisional) high-point and end-point: Zurich Concrete Art offered a safe harbour for those beset by worries and doubts, argued Martin Heller, the then charismatic chairman of the Swiss Werkbund. More pointedly still, he went on to suggest 'This art is a safe investment'.[4] In a continual stream of paintings, sculptures, silkscreen prints, multiples, posters and mass produced goods, the products of this movement percolated through enlightened Swiss living rooms and conquered the walls of banking and insurance boardrooms – not to mention the shelves of tasteful department stores. Heller concluded that Concrete Art was, to date, the Swiss art project with the greatest (boundlessly enthusiastic) mass appeal. Bill helped to promote this perception by presenting himself exclusively as a painter and sculptor in his exhibitions and publications in later years. The applied art, typography, poster design or 'product form' (the term he used in place of the English word 'design') now appeared marginal – mere spin-offs from his work in fine art.[5]

PS

Of course it is improper to reduce Max Bill (and his reception) to Concrete Art alone. And so it should be noted that concurrent with these reservations about Bill's art there was a renewed interest in Bill as an architect.[6] In the context of an emerging 'new simplicity' in architecture – evident in the early works of Peter Zumthor or Peter Märkli, say, or the office of Herzog & de Meuron (and exemplified in the use of so-called 'poor materials' or a reduced formal vocabulary) – the qualities of a programmatically unspectacular architecture such as Bill's acquired renewed relevance.[7] And as was impressively demonstrated by the comprehensive exhibitions devoted to Max Bill in Stuttgart, Zurich, Winterthur and Herfort in 2005 and 2008, the time was finally also ripe for a reassessment of his output as a whole – his work as a painter, sculptor, architect, graphic designer, typographer, critic, writer, publisher and educator.[8]

FROM THE BAUHAUS TO ULM

Bill himself summed up his career most concisely and pertinently under the rubric 'from the Bauhaus to Ulm'.[9] When Bill was young there were no art schools in Switzerland, so he started off as an apprentice silversmith in the School of Applied Arts in Zurich. A visit to the 1925 Paris Exposition Internationale des Arts Décoratifs et Industriels Modernes, along with a lecture by Le Corbusier organised by the Swiss Werkbund in Zurich in 1926, inspired his subsequent decision to become an architect and to enrol in the newly opened Dessau Bauhaus.[10] He spent just a year and a half there, but it laid the foundation for his future activities. At Dessau Bill not only gained experience in a range of artistic disciplines but also, and no less importantly, built up enduring contacts with many well-known figures in the avant-garde before he returned to Zurich, a 20-year-old artist crowned with the prestige of having studied at the Bauhaus. There he lived, keeping his head above water with small commissions for lettering or advertisements – modest things admittedly, but done with the assurance that he was now part of the international avant-garde. Following the pioneers of modernism that he knew personally – van Doesburg, Kandinsky, Klee, Albers, Moholy-Nagy, Vantongerloo, van de Velde and Le Corbusier – Bill set out to define an independent response to their achievements, one that was appropriate to his time. He later described his situation in this period in the following way:

Max Bill: Ulm stool, 1954. Courtesy max, binia and jakob bill foundation

Max Bill, 'Patria' typewriter, 1944. Courtesy max, binia and jakob bill foundation

the bauhaus became for me the epicentre, with its overlapping of disciplines and its insistence that in everything we design we have a personal responsibility towards society or, as the later formulation had it, the whole environment created by us, from the spoon to the city, had to be brought into harmony with social conditions, which implied shaping those conditions too.[11]

Shuttling between Zurich and the art capital of Paris, where he spent the 1930s in the circle around Michel Seuphor and Theo van Doesburg, Bill began to pursue new paths, initially in painting and sculpture. The result of this was the formulation of the principles of *konkrete gestaltung* (concrete design), a term originating with van Doesburg; this art, Bill wrote in 1936, 'arises out of its own means and laws, without these having to be derived or borrowed from external natural phenomena. the optical composition is based on colour, form, space, light, movement.'[12] From there Bill began to reformulate the entire field of the modern visual arts, from painting through sculpture, architecture, graphic design and typography to the applied arts.

In Bill's educational schema each discipline was to be treated in accordance with its own laws and techniques. A blurring of boundaries, as practised by Le Corbusier, was decisively rejected. For Bill, each design task had to be resolved with respect to the character of the specific medium and the function that was to be fulfilled. This basic principle, almost of necessity, engenders a plurality of forms. But in Bill's design practice one often finds the opposite: namely, formal themes are translated easily from one discipline into another and then back again.

Bill was given the opportunity to put his ideals into practice in 1950, when the Geschwister Scholl Foundation commissioned him to design both the curriculum and the building for the Hochschule für Gestaltung in Ulm. What he attempted there was not just an overlapping of disciplines, as at the Bauhaus, but an interplay within the framework of what he would eventually call 'environmental design'. More than that: for Bill, the modern culture of objects was to be expressed in the quasi-mathematical formula of form = beauty. The ideal situation, said Bill in the small exhibition catalogue conceived for the City Museum of Ulm in 1956, would be one where

all phenomena, from the smallest object up to the city, were in the same way the sum of all functions in harmonious unity = gestalt and thus a self-evident component of daily life. one would then be able to call this situation culture. that's what we're striving towards.[13]

The illustrated pages of the catalogue offered a pictorial representation of this concept of 'culture'. A kaleidoscopic array of Bill's work was reproduced in a uniform scale, at the size of postage stamps, depicting forms ranging from a power plug to a design for a memorial.

The aim of the Hochschule für Gestaltung, Bill's most important pedagogical experiment, was, quite simply, to shape a better postwar world. In contrast to the Bauhaus of the 1920s, what stood at the forefront of Bill's design theory in the 1950s was not the concept of function but rather the aesthetic aspect of form. Ultimately it was precisely this aspect of the education at Ulm that Bill's younger successors later considered too academic and rejected. As a result of this rejection Bill had to resign his post as rector of the school in 1956 and admit the failure of his plan to reshape design education.[14]

BEAUTY

For the generation of artists born after 1900, reconstruction was a central theme – even for those, like Bill, who had observed the war from a protected enclave. In the years after 1945 a particular importance was assigned to the Werkbund and its promotion of industrially produced consumer goods: these mobile objects represented a relatively quick means to build a new world – one that was better, more beautifully designed. Of course Bill had been engaged with the applied arts and industrial design for some time before he carried out his first commission in this field, the redesign of the 'Patria' typewriter in 1944. Further commissions (for chairs, tables, lamps, hairbrushes, mirrors and clocks) were to follow. But what turned out to be even more crucial than these objects – some of which remain very attractive and usable today – were the design reforms that Bill promoted under the banner of *Die gute Form*. These set standards far beyond the borders of Switzerland, so that Bill became a sought after guest speaker (for example at the International Design Conference organised by Walter Paepcke in Aspen, Colorado, among other places). The initial impulse came from a lecture, titled 'Beauty from Function and as Function' [see pp. 32–41, that Bill delivered at the 1948 annual conference of the Swiss Werkbund.[15] His theoretical pronouncements must have struck a nerve, because the association promptly commissioned him to bring the topic to a wider public with a practice-related design show. If, as we may assume, Bill himself was responsible for the exhibition title, *Die gute Form*, then he scored a major triumph with it. It was his idea not only to showcase exemplary products but also to launch an annual design award under the same label. This initiative, which lasted from 1952 right up to 1969, didn't just create a pithy brand name for the Swiss Werkbund. The idea was taken up outside Switzerland too, under appellations such as Good Design (Museum of Modern Art, New York) or Compasso d'oro (La Rinascente, Italy). Bill's extensively illustrated publication *FORM*, which appeared in 1952 in German, French and English, became (and is still considered today) a cult book of the 1950s.[16]

Bill's theoretical reflections on modern product design enacted a vital paradigm shift – they brought back into play the concept of beauty, which up to then had been excluded from modernist discourse. In opposition to a purely utilitarian aesthetic, Bill now declared formal quality to be a necessary part of the design. And he called for beauty to be treated on a par with function:

it has become clear to us that beauty can no longer be developed out of function alone; instead, the demand for beauty has to be set on the same level as a functional demand, since it is a function too.[17]

In contrast to the earlier Werkbund Bill did not promote truth to materials nor was he against handcrafts; rather his aim was 'an extreme utilisation of materials, where the maximum effect is achieved with the minimum of materials'.[18] With this Bill established an aesthetic of spare elegance. His thinking found such resonance because it synthesised demands for design reform with an impulse to create types and standards and a reconsideration of 'the artistic design of everyday objects'.[19]

WORDS

Measured against the enormous interest that Bill has attracted as a painter, sculptor, architect, graphic designer or teacher, Bill's written work seems to represent a blind spot in the topography of his all-embracing oeuvre. Yet he himself indicated the importance of this medium on several occasions: 'my activities as a commentator must be the hardest to represent, though they are often vital for understanding the rest of my work and the motives under-lying many things', was how he put it in the Ulm cata-logue.[20] The fact is that Bill's texts, criticism or theories run parallel to the other media in which he expressed himself, and so they should be examined in terms of whether Bill also used language in accordance with its own laws and principles. So, could we say that this language reached its ideal state when the sum of all functions in harmonious unity = *gestalt*, with its aims being expressed in economic mathematical prose: form, function, beauty = *gestalt*?

As Eugen Gomringer, a proponent of Concrete Poetry and a friend of Bill's, rightly noted, Bill 'time and again reached for language in order to report on motives and connections, not just in his own work but in that of others

Max Bill, study for type, film negative, 1960s. © DACS 2010

too'. [21] He attempted to do so with as much precision as possible, by creating and popularising expressions for thinking about and articulating artistic processes: 'Concrete Art', 'the mathematical approach in contemporary art', 'beauty from function and as function', 'good design' and 'from making to faking' are just a few of the emblematic tags that he attached, with a certain linguistic intuition, to his essays. Equally typically, if he found established orders of speech and thought outmoded, he would overturn them and build them up anew. The following collection of essays bears impressive testimony to this impulse. Gomringer sees Bill's great achievement as having been to 'stimulate an ordering of concepts within our metalanguage about art and "product form".' [22] Needless to say that Concrete Poetry, as Gomringer himself practised it, had developed in close dependence on Concrete Art. In Concrete Poetry language does not serve to describe a content, a thought or a mood, but itself becomes the aim and object of the poem. Yet Bill doesn't go this far. While his texts have an undeniable linguistic individuality, their meaning and function hardly reside in self-referentiality.

In his graphic or typographic works, however, Bill appears to pursue another principle. Here he was interested in creating word-images, in the optimal configuration of text and in the architecture of language. As early as the 1930s he developed a house typeface for the Wohnbedarf firm in Zurich and then extracted from this an individual character which was ultimately used as a self-contained artistic motif, not only in a graphic work but also in a relief. For a purely typographic poster for an exhibition of Concrete Art in 1944 Bill made hundreds of pencil sketches in order to achieve a universally valid subject as well as an optimal text figure. His exploration of language and its communicative potential went further still in the early 1960s, when Bill attempted to compose a whole typeface out of word-images. By emphasising the vowels, he intended to find a correspondence between the appearance of words and their acoustical form and so increase, in an almost industrial sense, the speed of reading. The typeface did not make it into production at the time, but in 1997 a digital version was produced, in both roman and italics.

Finally a word on lower-case type, which Bill used wherever and whenever possible after his return from the Bauhaus. (His heirs and the administrators of his estate continue to do so to this day.) This way of writing originated in attempts to reform the German language initiated in the 1920s by Walter Porstmann, the theoretician of standardisation and the founder of the German standard paper size, DIN A4. So it is rooted not in philological or philosophical considerations but in office management practices. At the Bauhaus Herbert Bayer and Josef Albers promoted it in a similarly economic spirit: 'we write everything small in order to save time'. The protagonists of the modern and their spiritual heirs, however, were not only thinking of greater ease of reading. The lower-case writing, like the new Akzidenz-Grotesk typefaces, symbolised the speed of the new means of communication and generally stood for an open, 'modern' approach to art and society. One of the most outstanding and successful artists in the postwar period, Bill was clearly aware not only of the function of words and the beauty of their forms but also of their media effect. Lower-case type thus became part of a personal trademark or label.

NOTES

1. A film from the time of the student unrest that is now only known to insiders, *22 Questions for Max Bill* (directed by Georg Radanovicz, 1968–69) shows sequences in which Bill's luxury automobile is presented as the pure antithesis of the monkish modesty of the Hochschule für Gestaltung in Ulm and thus as an aid to the crass filmic demolition of the artist.

2. The classic on this theme remains Serge Guilbaut, *How New York Stole the Idea of Modern Art* (Chicago, 1983). With regard to the consolidation of avant-gardism in the Swiss art system in particular see Hans-Jörg Heusser and Hans A. Lüthy, *Kunst in der Schweiz, 1890–1980* (Zurich, 1983), 61–67, and for the situation in the US see Max Kozloff, 'American Painting During the Cold War', *Art*

Forum, 1973, 43–54. A recent (as yet unpublished) text by Stanislaus von Moos, 'Kalter Krieg und neue Stadt' addresses the connections between Concrete Art and the Cold War.

3. Philip Ursprung devoted an inspiring essay to these connections, 'Continuity: Max Bill's Public Sculpture and the Representation of Money', in Charlotte Benton (ed.), *Figuration/Abstraction: Strategies for Public Sculpture in Europe 1945–1968* (Burlington, VT, 2004), 231–49.

4. Martin Heller, 'Unendliche Schleife des reinen Ausdrucks', in Ulrich Binder and Martin Heller (eds.), *Über Sicherheit und Zusammenarbeit* (Zurich, 1995), 134.

5. Stanislaus von Moos, 'Schönheit als Funktion: Anmerkungen zu Bill', in Arthur Rüegg and Ruggero Tropeano (eds.), *Wege zur 'Guten Form'*, *Rassegna* XVII, 62, 1995, 69.

6. See Hans Frei, *Max Bill: Konkrete Architektur?* (Baden, 1991) and a special issue of 2G, Karin Gimmi (ed.), *Max Bill: Arquitecto/Architect* (Barcelona, 2004).

7. *Minimal Tradition: Max Bill and The 'New Simplicity' 1940–1996*, exhibition catalogue for the Milan Triennale, with contributions by Stanislaus von Moos, Hans Frei and Karin Gimmi (Baden, 1996).

8. See the exhibition catalogues: Thomas Bruchsteiner and Otto Letze (eds.), *Max Bill, Maler, Bildhauer, Architekt, Designer* (Ostfildern-Ruit, 2005); *Max Bill: Aspekte seines Werks* (Sulgen, 2008); Marta Herford Museum, *Max Bill: Ohne Anfang ohne Ende* (Zurich, 2008).

9. Max Bill, 'vom bauhaus bis ulm', in *Du. Europäische Kunstzeitschrift*, June 1976, 13.

10. Documents on Bill's 18-month stay at the Bauhaus can be found in Jakob Bill's *max bill am bauhaus* (Bern, 2008).

11. Max Bill, 'vom bauhaus bis ulm', op. cit., 13.

12. Max Bill, 'konkrete gestaltung', in *Zeitprobleme in der Schweizer Malerei und Plastik*, exhibition catalogue, Kunsthaus Zürich, 1936, 9.

13. Max Bill, exhibition catalogue for the city of Ulm 1956.

14. Arthur Rüegg, 'Die Erziehung zum "bewussten menschen": Max Bill als Lehrer', in *Max Bill: Aspekte seines Werks*, op. cit., 90.

15. Max Bill, 'Schönheit aus Funktion und als Funktion', in *Werk* 8, 1949, 272–74.

16. Max Bill, *Form: Eine Bilanz über die Formentwicklung um die Mitte des XX Jahrhunderts. A Balance Sheet of Mid-Twentieth-Century Trends in Design. Un Bilan de l'Evolution de la Forme au Milieu du XXe Siècle* (Basel, 1952).

17. Max Bill, 'Schönheit aus Funktion und als Funktion', in *Werk* 8, 1949, 272.

18. Ibid., 273.

19. Stanislaus von Moos, 'Industrieästhetik', *Ars Helvetica* XI, Disentis 1992, 258.

20. Max Bill, exhibition catalogue for the city of Ulm 1956, 4.

21. Eugen Gomringer, 'Max Bill und die konkrete dichtung', in Eugen Gomringer (ed.), *Max Bill: Festschrift zum 50 Geburtstag* (Teufen, 1958), 56–62.

22. Ibid., 58.

Max Bill with the sculpture 'six-sided figure in space with sides of equal length'
(sechseck im raum mit gleichen seitenlängen), Atelierhaus Zürich-Höngg, 1947
(Photo Ernst Scheidegger) © Neue Zürcher Zeitung Photo

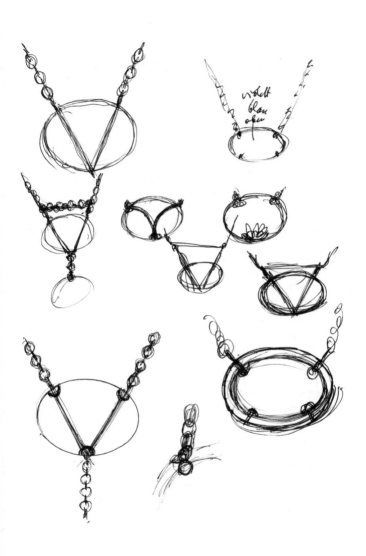

Sketches for necklace in yellow gold and opal

WHY I MAKE JEWELLERY
FROM TIME TO TIME (1945)

From time to time I design a piece of jewellery in response to either an internal impulse or, more rarely, an external commission. It may be that someone asks me for something, or perhaps I'll get an idea that can't be realised in any other form. When I make jewellery, it seldom involves a secondary motive – in contrast to the goldsmith, who has to earn his living from it. For me to take on something that wouldn't have come about in any case is an exception, and it happens only if someone asks me if I could draft something along the lines of some piece of mine that they've seen. But apart from this I make jewellery quite independently, simply as a small object that suits a person particularly well because they share the same underlying style. For me creating these pieces of jewellery is akin to creating a sculpture; they're just a smaller format. They're a kind of small object whose principal meaning lies in their form and their material. Whether this material is a precious stone set in gold or, in another case, polished glass in a chrome metal setting, or a found stone, has a bearing on the expression of the object, but its monetary value does not depend on costly material. Can you buy stones with very special kinds of markings? Never! You find them. Does a ring formed from a single filament, with no visible join, have to be made of gold? Hardly, because its content is the idea of the form and not its carat weight. I don't mean by this that the material is incidental. On the contrary, it is of the greatest importance. A beautiful gemstone, well cut and correctly set, has meaning too. But it doesn't just come down to cost; it's about the way the thing is formed, as with any other artwork whose value cannot be measured by its material alone. Something inconsequential does not become more beautiful when it's made of gold – it only becomes more expensive. This often comes to mind when you encounter jewellery ('adornment') whose sole interest is that you can gauge, from a single look, how much it cost to make, but instead of having a clear, meaningful, artistic form it appears as a pitiful jumble, only made out of precious metal and polished stones.

One could perhaps object that what I'm making hardly qualifies as jewellery, for jewellery should be adornment, rather than the independent vehicle for a formal idea. But what, then, do we understand by adornment? When it comes down to it, doesn't this mean signs and symbols? Otherwise, fresh flowers would surely be the only adornment we'd need!

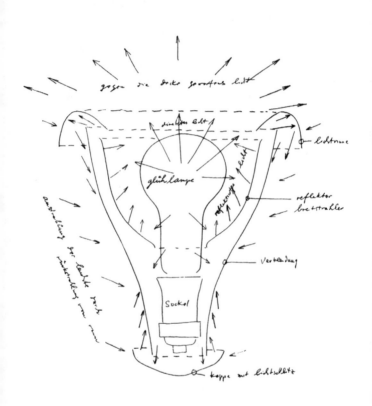

Sketch for indirect Lighting for Bag Turgi, 1944–46

MY EXPERIENCE OF PRODUCT DESIGN (1946)

For years we've been insisting on the need to create industrial standards for consumer goods, so that they are technically correct and correspond to some uncontrollable notion of what is 'beautiful' while at the same time meeting all the demands we make of them – technical and functional as well as aesthetic and social. We always have in mind an ideal picture when we think about these things, but it's difficult to define: if we were asked, we'd be hard pressed to name a single specific feature. Casting around for more concrete examples, we repeatedly return to a handful of standards, such as the products made by Dunhill (pipes, cigarette holders, lighters). But here too we find ourselves wondering about the last model that we saw – did it really correspond fully to our ideal image, did it match our optimum requirements? A few more examples then come to mind (some pieces of Lusatian glass, or various knives, or items of sports equipment) but when we compare them to the light fixtures that were once held up as exemplars of form and function (from the time of the Bauhaus or the heyday of the Deutscher Werkbund) reservations once again arise – a feeling that these things may once have been well meant and useful, but their time has passed.

Why they should not have withstood the test of time is much harder to say. Perhaps they were never quite as functional as they were made out to be. Perhaps they were more influenced by contemporary formalist tendencies than one wanted to admit, or suspected, at the time. And what about the furniture from that glorious era? Out of the plethora of models, what has remained useful or become a real standard? A small and dwindling number. And yet now and again you come across an object or appliance

that fulfils all your requirements, that is functional, true
to materials and formally beautiful, that you feel drawn to.
This might be a pair of gloves, for example, or a suitcase
or briefcase, a hammer or tongs, a standard wooden ladle
or stainless steel kitchen cutlery. It might be a tap or a door
handle that you find particularly pleasing to touch. But
when your own turn comes to make the most of a commission, everything looks a little different from your imagined
ideal picture. For example a client may come along and
expressly request a streamlined casing for a typewriter.
Even though the internal mechanism is taken from an existing model and is not itself new, it has to be covered with a
new shell. Not just for formal reasons, but to keep the dust
off – that much is self-explanatory.

The first thing you need to ask yourself with a
commission like this is whether you could (or indeed
should) take it on in the first place. In the end you resolve
to give it a try just this once. And when you do, you learn
that this model of typewriter is the only one of its kind,
the only one this firm makes – and that they intend to
manufacture it not just for the 1944 season, but unaltered
for years to come.

This means that streamlining is out of the question,
for all the things that got the client so excited – all the
American toasters, cars, ice boxes and kitchen appliances –
are just forms to cover up the mechanisms. They bear very
little relation to what really goes on inside, and are simply
an addition, a fashionably elegant touch designed to last
a single season.

You don't want to go there. So you talk the client out
of this grand streamlining scheme on economic grounds.
(Better not mention any artistic or moral reservations, as
that might just make him more determined to demand
the opposite of what you have in mind.) And you resign
yourself to making the simplest possible thing to accom-
pany the existing mechanism. You take in your stride all
the little levers that come with the machine and apply
yourself to ensuring that, despite everything, something
decent emerges.

But before that, there's a final set of hurdles to overcome – battles about the things that you find particularly important. For example, if you really don't want the space bar to be wedged between the two ends of the frame any more. Or if you particularly want to emphasise what is typical about the typewriter, the curve of the crown of type bars. These typical characteristics are precisely the things that make one model stand out from another – and the only way to distinguish between them as time goes on and these machines begin to look more and more alike.

A commission to design indirect lighting for office and commercial spaces is another thing altogether. We are all pretty well acquainted with this kind of indirect, diffused, non-glare lighting. Most fixtures consist of dark shades suspended from the ceiling that they illuminate. Which is generally seen as quite irritating. The point is to come up with an alternative.

When you look at what really lies beneath these shades, it becomes clear that in many cases the light bulb is housed in such a way that the distribution of light is undirected and far from optimised. One variation has a bulb with a mirror reflector directed so that it shines light on the ceiling, which makes good use of the light. But why then, you wonder, when the reflector casts the light onto the ceiling, does it still need that large shade? And you're astonished to realise that the sole reason for the shade's continuing presence is to conceal the neck of the bulb from view – something it never manages to do convincingly. Another option is to illuminate the dark shade from below, using the existing set up with both the suspended light bulb and the reflector covered by a large shade.

A further variation tackles the visible neck of the light bulb. The bulb is turned around and the lamp socket inserted at the base of the fixture, so that the reflector now beams its light unobstructed onto the ceiling. These functional components are cased in a harmoniously balanced form, with light slits in a cap at the base and a groove at the top. This adjustment makes the light fixture smaller; it's no longer a dark form hanging in the room, and it makes better use of the light. But already with these two objects we see how everything that we consider to be purely functionalist – or that might be called the 'technical style' – recedes far into the background, albeit without losing its fundamental importance. The main interest lies in giving an aesthetic shape to the functional form, or rather, perhaps, in shaping the form in such a way that it does not run counter to function but is as practical and as beautiful as possible. This is a matter of experience and judgement; it's about the harmonious line of a curve and the exact balancing of volumes and proportions, which are just as important as the pure function. And when you're doing all of this you mustn't be afraid to reach solutions that may at first seem strange – that don't turn out anything like you'd imagined, but precisely because of this display a certain anonymity, a universality.

Things become more difficult, however, when it comes to producing goods in which the taste of the consumer plays a much more decisive role, such as a hairbrush or shaving brush. For even a shaving brush requires a careful correlation of function, technique and form. Your initial good intention of making a single model for all purposes, with different finishes to suit all pockets, is scotched from the outset by the multiplicity of technical options. So you end up with four or five prototypes: all of them fulfil their purpose, but ultimately the one that is the most satisfactory technically and formally, as well as the most beautiful, also turns out to be the most expensive – and so a social ideal gets buried under a pile of sketches and variations. Even the cheapest model, however, is beautiful and good value.

As for the hairbrush, public taste comes into play long before you even begin, and even if you have no intention of making compromises, you can't be sure you're not doing so. But the core principle here remains the same: you have to omit everything that falls short of the optimum in terms of function, and make nothing that is less pleasing aesthetically than the most beautiful thing you can imagine of its kind. The sheer range of options and materials make the work more difficult and add to the confusion; you can do it this way – but equally you can do something else. It's not easy to work out a standard as you go, particularly as the manufacturing process is not always completely automated but depends to a large degree on the workers handling the machines. In such cases it's not very instructive to refer back to the most beautiful models, which reflect an attempt to define the curve down to the last tenth of a millimetre, to balance each refinement of the proportions. And yet you still cling to your hope that what will emerge will perhaps be better than what came before.

Experience shows that in the long run it pays manufacturers (and not just of luxury articles, but also of mass consumer goods) to have well-designed standard models that are perfected through continual fine-tuning.

If we consider the situation in Switzerland in particular, we can see that we are only able to compete in the world market by producing goods of exceptional quality. From this perspective, it is natural that our long-cherished principle of ennobling form is also being embraced by progressive industries and business operations today.

THE GOOD FORM (1949)

This exhibition [*Die gute Form*] highlights outstanding achievements in the most varied fields of human activity. It ranges from the simple observation of especially perfect natural forms, through the discovery of scientific truths, to expressions of artistic intuition – of a creative impulse which then finds its parallel in the application of natural laws to all sorts of technology, from machine components to household appliances to the sophisticated work-tools used by people today.

All of these forms arise from more or less exact thought processes. Most are based on extensive experience and are the outcome of long years of development. But this is not the case with all the objects that surround us, many of which are shaped by completely different motives. Development is not a linear process. Thus a stool – to take as an example one of our simplest, most essential use-objects – is not always determined by purely functional needs; in fact, whether any stool is truly functional in the real sense of the word – satisfying all the requirements for comfort and elegance while at the same time being affordable – is highly debatable. Meanwhile, stools are still being made in the form of ship's propellers, for example.

Curiously, the serviceability of a stool is harder to gauge than the increased efficiency of a new machine. Something else comes into play when we evaluate objects, and that something else is what is (rather generally) called 'beauty'.

There is an old saying that beauty is in the eye of the beholder, and that taste is a personal matter. But experience shows that it is perfectly possible to talk about taste. Some things are widely considered to be beautiful, others are seen as ugly. To some extent, this evaluation is tied to the age of the objects. With objects that are subject to technical change, ie whose function is not completely fixed, the form ages rather quickly. A telephone from 25 years ago may look like an oddity today. And a 40-year-old car comes across as a joke, unless you happen to be a vintage car buff admiring it from a technical viewpoint. At the beginning of the twentieth century, appliances like cookers or sewing machines were still quite primitive, and people felt they had to be decked with scrolls.

Items of furniture are a different matter, because their function is fundamentally unchanged and their development essentially complete, even if certain changes occur in their use and in the technical possibilities of manufacture. In such cases changes arise not on account of function but as a result of shifting tastes. The role of age is now reversed: what is old becomes beautiful: customs, nostalgia for the bygone splendour of the landed gentry, the yearning to return to the way things used to be, all become confused with the inherent value of the objects. The more ostentatious something is, the more people seem to want it. The striving for a higher station in life, the desire for social advancement, often finds expression in misguided extravagance. But isn't there also this saying 'appearances can be deceptive'? And isn't this borne out by experience? That's why we've tried in this exhibition to dispense as far as possible with 'appearance' and focus instead on what is modest, true – even good.

But now let's get back to taste – a disputed area – and to the fact that many other factors apart from taste determine the form of an object. One of these is the material employed, whether it is solid or unsound. Another is whether the object is practical or barely usable. Or whether it corresponds to its purpose perfectly, or only partially. Or obstructs space, or frees it up. Or how much it costs in relation to its true value, ie whether it's good value or overpriced. These are all rational arguments that we take into account when we buy an object, or at least that we ought to factor in; and together these arguments shape our perception of quality. We learn from experience that quality is never cheap, though it turns out to be the cheapest option in the long run, and that its outer form is mostly simple, low-key. If we do not take these qualities into account when making our purchases, we are led by something else: namely by the way things look, their external appearance. But just because something looks expensive, it doesn't necessarily mean it has any value. A sleek veneer tends to conceal a lack of true quality. True quality is usually defined by an unostentatious elegance. So we're right to mistrust the outer appearance, which can take on a number of guises – which can lie. These guises are not just plucked from the past, they don't only mimic historic styles from the gothic to constructivism: there's also a contemporary version of this masquerade – the streamlined style. And there are good grounds for mistrusting this too. It's a fashion that bears as little relation to contemporary realities as a historic style. Streamlined, or empire style – both are equally ridiculous when applied to a pram. Both would have the pram appear as something other than it really is. Both lie.

By contrast, what our exhibition aims to present are projects that are sincere and in keeping with the spirit of our times. We're fully aware that things of perfection are rare. Propelled by vanity, people can't leave a simple thing alone, but always have to add something to make it stand out. When this is done with a measure of skill and good judgement, we begin to believe that it's possible to add a touch of individuality, of, let's say, artistic intuition – that it's possible to take an object of straightforward construction and make it beautiful too, consciously beautiful. But things like this are even rarer than things which fulfil their purpose in a good, straightforward way: ie machines, work-tools, appliances. Hence we can already consider ourselves fortunate if the objects that we use everyday are useful in the same manner as work-tools, rather than counter to reason. Some may object that such expectations are not realistic, that people are not rational but will always judge things according to their own ill-defined notion of taste. Yet experience teaches us that this is not quite the case. Though we know that habits change only slowly, we can nevertheless observe a gradual shift in taste occurring over time, so that many things that might have been thought beautiful 40 years ago are now seen as ridiculously florid and overdone. Equally, many of the things that might appear experimental today will tomorrow seem quite normal.

It is often asked whether we should continue to make things in the time-honoured manner, or alternatively convert wholesale to 'industrial' production. This question is only of hypothetical interest. Our concern here is to make available to a large number of people things that are as beautiful as they can be – as well as good value. Both traditional crafts and industry are in a position to fulfil this wish, since there is in principle no difference between these manufacturing techniques when it comes to producing quality. If the focus here is almost exclusively on furnishing objects, it's because these are of particular concern to the Swiss Werkbund. No less important, however, are buildings: they have to last even longer, and accommodate us happily for many years. The face of our cities, our towns and villages, our landscape is likewise a concern, for this bears witness to our era's capabilities – or lack of them – not only today and tomorrow but for generations to come.

So if we've tried to allude to all of these issues in our exhibition by presenting selected, complementary examples from the most diverse creative fields, we've done so out of a desire to highlight the forces that are making a positive contribution to shaping the face of the present. And in closing with the remark that the future will judge our time in the same way that we judge the past – that is, according to the character of its culture and the cultural level it has reached, as well as by its social achievements – we wish to say that we have to guard against the danger of going by appearances and instead attempt to bring all our contemporary powers into a harmonious balance – into what we'd like to call 'the good form'.

BEAUTY FROM FUNCTION
AND AS FUNCTION (1949)

For around a hundred years now the call to action has sounded in successive waves throughout the world: we have a duty to make useful, ethical products that are true to materials and manufactured under socially responsible conditions, using the best means available to us. Inherent within this call is a sense of moral responsibility, a social understanding. Yet in almost every case this is not so much the starting point as the post-rationalisation for a distinctly artistic process. A closer look reveals that the initial impulse arises not so much from a conscious feeling of responsibility towards the user as from a sense of responsibility for the form, from the constant will to define a new expression. The concept of social responsibility is something that artists and others deploy after the event, as a way of justifying their search for new forms responding to new or changed conditions.

And that's how it has remained up to the present day, to some extent in technology as well. New forms that are perceived to be artistic arise not out of a pure sense of responsibility towards the eventual user, but out of a more universal need to give things form. This does not mean, of course, that social factors are not taken into account in the design; it's just that such considerations haven't yet been the basis for creating anything.

And so we've reached the point where every change in form – and not just those which can be seen from season to season and influence everyday use-objects as well – can be characterised as a change in social practices and therefore, broadly, as fashion.

Now the Werkbund has always been associated with the idea of 'truth to materials'. But when we ask ourselves what this phrase really means, it's hard to come up with definitive answer. We discover that truth to materials depends very much on the fulfilling of function. On the other hand, as everyone knows, almost any form can be produced from almost any material, and it's impossible to say categorically that one variant is 'true' and the other 'false'. To give an example: is it being true to materials to insist that plain ceramics should be of perfect quality when we know this is hard to achieve in terms of production, and certainly much more expensive than the standard process which allows for minor, inconsequential technical flaws?

This makes us realise that what we're actually striving for is something quite different – namely, an extreme utilisation of materials, where the maximum effect is achieved with the minimum of materials. For example, we can construct a tower 300 metres high (the Eiffel Tower) and make it so light (as Eiffel did) that if its height were reduced by a factor of one thousandth, ie by 30 centimetres, then its weight would drop by just seven grams – the weight of a pencil. This is a shining exemplar of the extreme exploitation of materials, an emblem for the technical age and the rational use of materials, as well as the germ of a new ideal of beauty. This coupling of the engineer's rationalism with beauty in construction – or 'rational beauty', as Henry van de Velde put it in his day – is the banner under which we must regroup when considering how to tackle production both now and in the future.

Beauty from function – which we still consider an essential codeterminant of beauty as function – is a phenomenon most readily observed when functions are brought to light in the purest way, without sentimental frippery, that is, in the construction of machines and tools, in the work of the engineer, though even here we can observe that forms often change in response to contemporary tastes while the functions remain the same.

This fact – that engineered forms change not only in response to changes in function but also for aesthetic reasons – is evidence of the tight correlation between beauty from function and beauty as function. Regrettably, however, this aesthetic insight seems barely to have penetrated the parallel field of everyday use-objects.

For years we've been asking how this has come about. For years, for generations now, the Werkbund has been stating its demands clearly, with less than satisfactory results. You have to search long and hard to find a simple, functional and beautiful chair, beautiful crockery, a functional, all-purpose door handle, a functional and beautiful lamp. It has become clear to us that beauty can no longer be developed out of function alone; instead, the demand for beauty has to be set on the same level as a functional demand, since it is a function too.

If we place particular value on something being beautiful, it's because pure functionality, in its narrow sense, is not what concerns us in the long term. We should no longer have to demand functionality – it ought to be a matter of course. But beauty is less self-evident, and ideas about what is beautiful or not beautiful often differ. That's why it's easier to keep on calling for functionality. The pursuit of beauty is much more difficult; it requires a greater effort, and succeeds only under particular creative conditions, when the idea of form meshes harmoniously with the particular task in hand. The two preconditions for this are first, the right commission, and second, the competence to design.

Let's first consider the commission before moving on to the question of the competence to design.

We all know that commissions have the potential to oppress. When we're given a brief to design something with a 'classic' status – for example, the constant tea cup, the one true chair, the definitive coffee pot, the folding step that can be deployed in any situation – we're fully aware of the relative nature of our products' claims to 'eternal' value. But it would be remiss of us to lessen our efforts to achieve the definitive result – or what corresponds at that moment, under those particular conditions, to our ideal of beauty – just because we know that, no matter what, this ideal is bound to change. We know that in every area of the production of use-goods, which includes the house itself as well as cars, trains and ships, there are an infinite number of projects that we could apply ourselves to with the aim of making something better and more beautiful than the things that already exist.

A great deal of effort has already gone into spelling out to manufacturers the need for beautifully designed products. We do not distinguish here between the hand-crafted and the industrially manufactured product, since both require our input. If we nonetheless place an emphasis on industrial goods, it's because these are manufactured in larger quantities and so have a much greater cultural impact than one-off pieces. However, when we come to take stock of what our efforts have achieved up to now, it seems we've made little progress.

The reason for this lies partly in the nature of the Swiss economy. In making his decisions the Swiss manu-facturer tends to have one eye on fashion trends abroad and the other on his immediate economic situation. In times of full employment he is reluctant to introduce new models, since this would disrupt the manufacturing process – even though this is precisely the moment he could afford to do so. When business is slow, on the other hand, he feels less committed to maintaining the technical quality of his products. Socially responsible manufacturers now have the possibility – indeed even the duty – to make products that are exemplary not only technically but also formally. But it has to be said that very few of them have given any thought to this, and despite our efforts many wouldn't even know where to begin to tackle this problem.

I believe that the path the Werkbund has pursued up to now is perhaps not the right one, since we've failed to reach the people that matter in Switzerland. I believe we could get better results from the approach, proposed a long time ago, of showcasing the cultural aspects of production in exhibitions of exemplary products at trade fairs. This would increase awareness in influential circles. As you know, the Leipzig fair put on exhibitions of this kind for many years, and they worked well because manufacturers saw it as an honour to have their products selected for a showcase for quality, run by people who knew what they were doing.

Finally, I have a few more remarks to make on the question of who is qualified to create industrial products. The past few years have seen the emergence of a new profession, the 'industrial designer', as they call it in Anglo-Saxon countries (where it's more prevalent than it is here, in some cases taking on corporate dimensions). Much of what these designers produce looks very attractive, and is superficially modern, but the design is often substandard, wantonly frivolous, with the fine facade concealing technical problems. A new style is being propagated and mass-produced: it is being 'streamlined'. So today's streamlined car bodies are in many cases the product of pure formalism, while insights that were ignored for many years (while Paul Jaray still had a patent on their pure form) are now being embraced for the sake of fashion. The result: the production of inflated tin cans – massive, but not significantly more comfortable – that are already shrinking our streets and parking places in a most unpleasant way. From cars it's a short step to extending this 'streamlining' to household appliances, prams and radios. But thankfully this epidemic has barely touched Swiss industry.

Here in Switzerland everything proceeds at a slightly more leisurely pace. For a start, things of beauty tend to be viewed with some suspicion in our puritanical and censorious land. But it can hardly be assumed this will always be so. Sooner or later developments that start abroad begin to percolate into Switzerland. The 'industrial designer' will arrive here too: just as the commercial graphic designer evolved from the painter who engaged with graphics into the independent profession of today, so the industrial designer will evolve out of necessity. But going by the dispiriting examples we've seen from abroad, these designers pose a substantial threat to our chances of checking the move towards superficiality. That is why we also have to ask: how do these designers enter the profession, and what demands should the Werkbund make of them?

Let's consider why industrial designers might be a good thing: mass production has to ensure not only that a certain beauty arises from the function of consumer goods, but that this beauty in itself becomes a function. In the future, mass-market consumer goods will be the barometer for a country's cultural standing. The designers of these goods will ultimately be responsible for a large part of our visual culture, just as architects are responsible for the healthy development of our cities and living places. The kind of practice we envisage, with its vast range of responsibilities, requires us to make quite different demands of the industrial designer than were made, for example, of applied arts practitioners in the early days of industrialisation. We are facing an educational problem which is perhaps not very significant on an individual level, but is exceptionally important in terms of its cultural impact – an educational problem that we'd scarcely begun to address at the time of the Bauhaus and that is hardly resolved today. There are no schools giving people the kind of education that we require today, no schools producing people that we could employ without reservation for this important task.

In Switzerland, to date, there has not been a single move in this direction. Even if you are of the opinion that our technical colleges (*Gewerbeschulen*) and schools of applied arts (*Kunstgewerbeschulen*) are potentially the right kind of institution, it has to be said that they're quite unsuited to this role in their current form. Since the education provided by a technical college has broadly to comply with Swiss laws on the training of apprentices, it's not much different from a practical apprenticeship, and there are plenty who maintain that the education they offer is wanting.

But if on-the-job training is in many cases more or less equivalent to completing a course at college, what's the point of college? What can it offer that's special, as opposed to widely available? The crafts taught in colleges today appear somewhat contrived, and only specialist subjects, suitable for those pursuing vocational training, seem to be authorised. But schools of industrial arts that work with a curriculum that is not substantially different from vocational training have lost their primary function, the purpose they were set up for, which is to point the way forward for progressive industry.

I've already remarked that there's essentially no difference between industry and handcraft, that the machine is a tool in the same way that a hammer is, for example – these are simply the prostheses we create to implement our work. Nonetheless, there is still a large manual element in what we call industrial production. Ostensibly technical products continue to be made using craft-based methods. So if I reproach the schools of industrial arts for still being rooted in the crafts, I'm not saying that they should ignore these techniques, but rather that they're not thinking enough about industry.

I believe there's no need to reiterate why industry is so important today. Unless you're cut off from reality you can't fail to see that in the long term industrial development offers not only a means of freeing people from the burden of heavy labour but also a huge opportunity for cultural development. Clearly, both of these things have yet to come about, but if we want to develop our cultural potential we need to have competent people making these industrial products – hence the necessity to educate this kind of designer. This represents a major challenge for our schools of industrial arts, not in their current form and with their current curriculum, but more as the foundation for something new. Based on my experience, I will briefly sketch out what such an education ought to look like.

Student numbers have to be kept very low. The prerequisite for study should be the completion of a technical apprenticeship, or possibly an equivalent course at a school of industrial arts, with a final examination in a technical subject. Students would not only get a comprehensive training giving them an insight into all the related professions, and with this a feeling for new materials, they'd also get a general education encompassing theory and practice in all fields of design as well as the basic concepts of statics, mechanics and physics. They would have to work with all kinds of material, not only theoretically but also in practical exercises carried out in workshops under appropriate supervision; in short, on top of their basic craft-based training they would receive a very complete artistic, technical and intellectual education. It is clear that such an institution cannot be constructed along the same lines as existing schools of industrial arts but has to be much more a kind of hybrid between an academy and a polytechnic, as the Bauhaus set out to be. A much greater emphasis, however, has to be placed on the development of personality: what we need are designers who are not just technically knowledgeable but are also true artists, uninfected by the idea that painting or making sculptures is somehow more important or of greater value than making perfectly beautiful, good industrial products. Once the production of mass-market consumer goods is in the hands of people like this we will be able to say that the cultural epoch of the machine age has truly begun. But until then, everything will remain piecemeal, at the mercy of chance.

So while we have to acknowledge, with regret, that our efforts have not yet yielded substantial results and large-scale production has not yet reached the standard we'd hoped for, we also have to accept that it will not be so easy to reach this standard any time soon, given the lack of an appropriate skills base.

To reiterate: our future industrial designers should not see their work as being less valuable than that of painters or sculptors. This does not constitute a declaration of war on the fine arts, for just as the latest discoveries in theoretical physics are ultimately indispensable for the production of simpler, more practical appliances that are of greater use to everyone, so the fine arts are indispensable for the development of all sorts of objects, and it is absolutely essential to grapple not only with the art of the past but also with the latest contemporary issues. Doing so will give a certain stylistic cohesion to all our diverse efforts, a unity between the latent formal tendencies and the explicit and unequivocal function of fine art, which is to bring forth perfect beauty, unimpaired by external constraints or restrictions. In this context, art also gives us a glimpse of the possibilities and questions, both positive and negative, that are in the air at any one time. Confronting these problems of design, which are now presenting themselves in an acute form, is not only essential in the production of use-objects, it's also an existential question of the first order for architecture. Unless it engages positively with these questions – and goes beyond treating mural painting and sculpture as decorative accessories – architecture, just like industrial design, will never get beyond a primitive stage of satisfying needs and will instead lose its way in historicist and artistic games.

In all kinds of things – appliances, shoes, technical tools or contemporary artworks – we can see a certain stylistic unity begin to emerge. This does not depend on the addition of external elements, in contrast to the 'style' envisaged by one particularly doughty housewife when she lectured Adolf Loos on the subject: 'if the bedside table has a lion's head on it and this lion's head also features on the sofa, the wardrobe, the beds, the armchairs, the washstand, in short on all the objects in the room, now that's what you call style'. But that's not the kind of style I mean: what I'm talking about is something that arises out of a disciplined, purposeful approach to design. We can draw a certain satisfaction from much of what we're doing today, and while concrete results may still be thin on the ground, there are enough of them to give us hope that the path we've embarked on is not misguided, and that this development will ultimately lead somewhere. These results also show that our thesis, which is now being taken up with renewed vigour, can be the basis for building a new culture that corresponds to our potential and our aesthetic conceptions. That this will need time to come about is something that has become clear to us over the course of the years.

Our efforts today have to go in two directions: first, into making manufacturers aware of the issues and increasing their sense of cultural responsibility, and secondly, into giving suitably talented individuals an education that will allow them, as industrial designers, to draw on their own experience, their own outlook and their own sense of responsibility to create things that we will be happy to use all the time, everyday – all kinds of things from a sewing needle to the arrangement of a house, and all of them guided by a spirit of beauty which is developed from function and which, through its beauty, fulfils its own function.

a, b, c, d… (1953)

from 1930 onwards, max bill wrote all his texts in lower case. this lecture was originally delivered in english.

ladies and gentlemen,

forgive me, if i speak to you about very important problems – i am thinking about problems of worldwide importance for the culture of our time, the time of machinism – using the vocabulary of a four-year-old child and the complex sentences of my own invention. maybe such an undertaking is a source of a lot of misunderstanding, but i have to take this risk since i cannot change it.

it would have been easy for me to translate one of my premade speeches or articles. but i hate to prepare speeches without knowing the special circumstances under which i will make this speech. here, the conditions are really new ones for me. i have never been to the states before.

i am coming from switzerland. our conditions are very different from yours. i thought I knew a great deal about american problems in the field of design, art and culture, because i read about these problems from time to time. but i realise that all this knowledge is very theoretical, and not based on own experience. so for this reason i could not come here with a premade speech. i could only give mr lionni a general title, 'art, business, culture, design'; this title includes all the problems i want to speak to you about.

before coming to the states i was in germany. we are just starting a school there, following bauhaus principles. just these days, we are beginning to construct the buildings, and in a few weeks we shall start to work with the first group of students. in germany i saw that they have other problems than in switzerland, because problems of production in general are different. then we went to brazil.

we had been invited there by the government to advise on educational problems in the field of architecture, art and design. this was my first contact with absolutely other conditions than european ones. i saw that countries without the whole history of style, without the tradition of an old craftsmanship need other things than europe and that all these problems must be settled on their own particular ground. then we went to peru and observed similar problems to brazil.

now we are in the states. here again it is a little different. i know a lot of old friends working here and i have seen your top architecture and design reviews. we have also had exhibitions of modern architecture and design in switzerland, we are in contact with museums of your country. but when we arrived a week ago in miami and saw for the first time the gardens and houses from the airplane, i got a new impression of the problems in your country. these houses, all individual, each one built to a high level and an agreeable standard, tell me that the influence of modern architecture on industrialised buildings, on the building business itself, is more important than i'd thought. nearly every one of the houses that i saw from the plane had a certain perfection and looked well designed. that means they are useful houses, they are well placed. however, i do not want to say that they are perfect, or that they could not be done better. and from above i saw just one of your big problems: the urban organisation. as the town is getting bigger and bigger, it is losing its structure, new settlements have no core... the next example i saw, also from the plane, was houston and, some time later, dallas. there were always the same problems, very easy to see from above ... a certain decentralisation. in between the structureless settlements were bigger buildings: schools, department stores and so on. but they're not too well organised, there's wasted space in the centre of the town just for parking lots. these problems are the same the world over. then we landed in denver. this town never existed for me before. i did not realise its importance. we crossed large, partly nice suburbs with lawns between the

houses and the streets, with no dividing line to the neigh-
bour's garden. it all looked very clean and, because
of the trees in between, it seemed to me agreeable to live in.
i saw a lot of different designs. what i had always seen in
journals as single houses now became a general aspect of
great variety and, finally, all of these houses are the
expression of the tendency to sell to the customer something nice and perhaps useful. this is not to deny that
without the help of an architect you could never live under
such agreeable circumstances in europe as in one of these
mostly prefabricated houses.

then, in the centre of denver, we saw for the first
time shops, show-rooms in which had been assembled all
those things i'd never thought could really exist. show-
windows filled with the most ugly things – crazy hats and
shirts, ties with photographic pictures of cowboys and
horses in full colour, horrible, crude jewellery. then i looked
at pottery, glassware, all those things we need everyday.
everywhere there was the same catastrophe: one department store only showed 'hardoy chairs', but in a very poor
imitation.

i cannot say that i saw everything that could be seen
in denver. however, i have the impression that all around
it would be quite the same. i won't deny that i saw some
good architecture, such as the hotel in which we stayed.
the facade was well constructed, composed of bricks, glass-
walls and windows, without a special style; the interior,
on the contrary, was very common. then some buildings
in the centre of the town could also be considered
as examples of good nineteenth-century architecture.
certainly much better than many new ones.

with this impression we came to aspen and are
meeting here, all of us interested in design. i thought that
we're all more or less crazy to have the idea to transform
the aspect of the products of our time. we are perhaps
wrong in our ideals, and people may never agree with our
creations. perhaps people do need decoration and ugly
things. but do they really need gadgets, in every kind of
styling, cowboy or streamlined?

are these really the questions of our time? what is
our function in this time? shall we really do silly things
for people? what is the function of the designer, of an
artist, today?

in order to settle some of these questions i will follow
the alphabet of the title of my speech: a, b, c, d: art,
business, culture, design. i will add another quartet: action,
brain, creation, decoration.

first i shall explain to you what i understand by
art, business, culture, design, and what the subtitle –
action, brain, creation and decoration – has to do with the
main one.

i define the notion of 'art' as the 'expression from an
individual being adequate to the most advanced knowledge
and feeling of his time', and i limit this to the plastic arts
'with the medium of light, space, movement'. but perhaps
this is not very complete, what does it mean?

1. 'the expression from an individual' means that
every creation on a high level, including art, is an
individual process. this does not mean that it is an
individualistic process like self-expression. art always
makes sense only as an objective creation of general
ideas. and this is the very difference between individual and individualistic. the individual is a part of
society and feels responsible not only for himself, but
for the whole. that means that his work, in *this* case, a
work of art, must be as objective, as clear, as meaningful as possible. the individualist does not feel responsible for society, his work will be self-expression
because he lives by the fallacy that his own person is
of the greatest importance.

2. 'being adequate to the most advanced knowledge
and feeling of his time': this means giving form to all
of those advanced ideas which cannot be explained in
any other way than by artistic inspiration. so the artist
has to create new symbols to explain the feeling for
things coming in the future. this is one important

function of art, and the task of an artist. the second one is to give harmony to life. you see, my definition is not closed in itself, it always at the same time comprises the relation between art and human being. what i've proposed is a high programme. it includes, no more nor less, the formation of the whole life of everyday. this means that it ultimately includes not just what we understand by plastic arts, indeed not just everything that is generally considered as fine arts. i limit once more the notion of 'art', using the concept 'concete art'. this concrete art is the opposite of abstract art … it is the realisation of abstract ideas in the world of concrete things. on the way to creation, abstract ideas become really visible and sensible. we have eliminated every parasite in painting and sculpture. by parasites, i mean objects of every kind and formation or deformation such as naked women, or men on horseback, landscapes, still-lifes and all of those things which today may better be taken with the camera. all of those things we like in reality, but not as parasites in so-called 'works of art'. that does not mean that artists no longer have an interest in the real world of objects and subjects. on the contrary, artists must take responsibility for the real world: for objects, creating things for everyday use; for subjects and their psychic and social health. works of art have an influence on everybody's mind if they are in the environment of men. objects for use as well as art objects form the environment, together with nature. the whole environment is of great importance for human health, and artists are responsible for it.

3. 'with the medium of light, space, movement' means, to be a little bit more exact, that the medium expressing an idea in the form of an artwork will be light – that is colour, clearness and shadow; it also means space, whether two-dimensional on the surface, or three-dimensional as volume or line in space, or four-dimensional as the movement of light,

volume and line in space. ultimately, art is an order, a prototype of harmony. every artist has to establish an order and a method for his expression; for every work he has to limit the infinite possibilities. this certainly is characteristic of every artistic expression, especially with respect to concrete art. in particular it is the artist who is responsible for the harmony in the life of our mechanised century. we hope that art will be no longer a surrogate for everyday life, but its source.

to art, i have connected 'action'. the sense of this is that art must become active, become action itself. art is not something pleasant without function, not something for decorating the walls or putting in a museum. art is action. a painting is a field of forces, a mixture of different tensions and, finally, this field of tensions is all the time producing new forces like a power-station. whether these forces are good or bad is the artist's responsibility. he is responsible for the actions of his works. however, action in this case cannot be understood only as the action of a work of art, but as the action of the artist himself, because his life is action against non-activity.

after all, i must emphasise that neither form, nor colour, nor idea, nor action, nor even their combination can by itself create a work of art or a design. what counts is only the result, and in regard to this the way the artist treats his problems – how his imagination finds out his manner of expression – is of greater importance than any other part of the process leading to the result. again, only the result counts and its effect on human beings.

what about 'business', the second letter of the alphabet? i think that business is neither good nor bad, but often it is on the wrong side of trade. unfortunately, business is frequently much more interested in waste than in the production of really good things for a longer period of use. in this way, business in the field of art is always dangerous, for works of art are becoming commercial objects, and so artists are becoming producers, which is of great danger for their artistic development. i believe business is overestimated today, because everybody needs money and for this reason moral questions have little appeal, but i can imagine that in a few years business in today's sense will no longer have the same importance. that is the question of production, above all, of the production of well-designed goods with a longer life, goods without the anticipation of waste. on the one side, this is a question of production, of better production with an excellent quality of execution.

on the other hand, we will come to a time when the production of energy will be changed: today, we are exploiters of the natural sources of the world's energy. men first had to use wood for getting fire, then coal formed from old sunken forests, then oil, coming from the bodies of the organisms of the primitive time of our earth. finally, we started to produce electric energy with the help of water, coal, oil. the period of exploiting these so-called natural energy sources will very soon change as we enter the nuclear age. this will completely change the techniques and at the same time will produce many more facilities for human life. the only barrier between this development and the welfare of the public might be business.

by this I mean that business might work against public welfare, because production capacity is so big and it must become bigger and bigger with the media of propaganda, advertising and things like that. and right there is the danger. machines are no longer a help for human beings, but dictators. instead of liberating men from tiring and long work, which could and should be the result of machinism, there is a danger of everything being turned over to a bad mass-production of short-lived things and every kind of gadget. instead of health and public welfare, we would then have haste and nervousness. business, industry, production would exist with very little moral background. responsibility would not exist. that would be a really lousy world to live in.

in a world like this, there will break out hate and political distress, communism and fascism, the twins of horror which limit our possibilities as human beings. under these circumstances, business hopes to win. but it is a miscalculation. business ultimately can only exist in connection with public welfare and progress. but today it seems that business is against progress, or progressive only in those cases where it is necessary to knock down the competition. i hope that the nuclear age will not just produce more gadgets, but will really bring the liberation of humanity. judging from today's situation, we can say that a lot of the things that are wrong in the world come from the business side.

of course a few institutions and some producers are not typical cases, but are perhaps forerunners of a future development: for example the activities of the container industry in your country, or big foundations like rockefeller or the ford foundation, or in europe the olivetti typewriter company ... if we look for the reason why these companies or corporations are going other ways, we find very quickly that they are led by personalities who have wider than purely commercial interests. they are not only interested in art and design, but in public welfare too. if we take for example the olivetti company, we find that adriano olivetti not only built very progressive factories a long time ago, but also houses for his workmen. he is producing not only machines of perfect design, but is running stores and publicity in a leading manner; however, this is not all, he is financing a series of different cultural journals of social interest, like *urbanistica*, the italian review of planning and town-planning; *communità*, a review of social and political problems as well as cultural problems in all fields of human activity, really a very progressive review. then *metron*, a review of architecture, and *sele arte*, an art review, a little bit in the direction of the late *magazine of art* in the states, which won't appear any more because – it is a shame – they are out of money. but this is not all, every month editione communità publishes a few books in the field of politics, economics, art, literature. i mention these examples to tell you that business, if it supports progress, is not only a helpful instrument for the production of useful things, but at the same time a help for the general progress of society.

what will be the result, if these few forerunners are

joined by more and more industries and the products they manufacture become better and still better in design and quality, and productivity becomes greater and greater and technical equipment fulfils every need? a time will begin when every man has freedom and can live under conditions that enable him to develop his knowledge and his abilities in a free society. if we fight for this freedom, and if we, as artists, create symbols for such freedom in a kind of infinite space, then we have to pay a price for this freedom, too … we have to liberate ourselves from a purely materialistic thinking. in the future, when problems of production and energy are settled, when plenty of useful and nice things are available for everybody, when forces are free to reorganise our towns and large parts of the devastated earth, thus building a big garden, then we shall get freedom and health. the price we have to pay for this is small: we only have to turn our attention from business to public aid. i do not think that an intervention by the state is necessary for such a development. the day will come when industry, business and production can no longer concentrate their interest only on money-making, when 'money-making' will automatically become nonsense, because everybody will be able to cover his expenses by working less since production will be so well organised and machines will be useful instruments and no longer dictators. that is not only an economic and a political question, above all it is a moral question. if we are against communism, we cannot fight it with fascism, but we can fight both with freedom and economic security. i was talking about the price we have to pay: there it is – to renounce voluntarily several monopolistic privileges. in the immediate future, businessmen must become leaders for freedom, and for this reason i have added as second notion to business: 'brain'. the transformation between the present manner of living and a future harmony in life can only be reached by thinking. and, for that purpose, men have a brain to think.

we have a brain not only to think about new inventions for industry, or general philosophical problems; above all we have it to think about our existence and how to make it better. if we use our brain in this way, all of the money-making business becomes nonsense and human intelligence can create things to help and serve and not to exploit. we must use our brain and think of the terrible situation we are living in as society, and of what a ridiculous situation we are in, the 'kings of the beasts', with all of our troubles and little extravagances, with our wasting time for nothing – ie in producing things we can never really use. we lost the natural life, we lost harmony, we lost freedom, but we have business. these are no longer humane living conditions and this is the bad side of industrialisation. but now, at the start of a real industrialisation, in which automation is a useful help to men, we must use our brain in building up new living conditions, those of the future, of a free society.

in this way we come to notion 3, 'culture'. by culture i understand 'a state in which power, knowledge and science is used to the best of human development'. power for construction and play, not for destruction. powder for fireworks, not for guns. electricity never for chairs, under no pretext. knowledge for public welfare. science to achieve more and more facilities for life and for the pleasure of the human mind. all that is culture. and it is also harmony in life on a high level, as high as it is possible in our time with our infinite possibilities. culture is what gives value to life. under these conditions, creation will be of greatest importance.

and now i shall explain to you what i understand by the second word beginning with a 'c', 'creation': 'creation is an act of man's intelligence and inspiration'. creation is neither good nor bad, but in every case is indispensable for progress. for me, creation has nothing to do with crazy inventions, it is something reasonable.

and next we come to the fourth of the notions, 'design': 'design is the process by which useful things are given the most beautiful and effective form, considering overall the function of these things'. you see, i limit the signification of design. i do not speak about all things drawn up and produced according to a design. i am speaking about useful things, and i believe that one of the most important arguments in design is use. useful things are those which are around us every day.

i explained under 'art' that the environment is of primordial importance for human welfare. so the responsibility of the designer is especially great. overall it is a moral one. he is responsible for the physical environment of men; he is able to make the world crazy and sick, or to bring in harmony. here, at this point, i want to remember the great moralists of modern design. there is henry van de velde, who, as a painter, came to design when he built a house with all new furniture. he did not want his children to grow up in an ugly environment. van de velde became one of the greatest pioneers of the modern movement before 1900, and a lot of his early writings can still be read today with great pleasure. two months ago, we celebrated his 90th birthday with him. he will always have his place in the front-line of the fight for good and valuable design. then adolf loos, who wrote many important things about design, and i especially remember his essay on ornament and crime where he speaks about the common sources of ornament and criminality – perhaps with a little bit of exaggeration, but the core of his explanations is as right today as it was 40 years ago.

i also remember another of these pioneers: walter gropius, who built up the famous bauhaus which gained influence all over the world and had above all a moral background. many parts of the bauhaus doctrine were powerful influences on education and industry, design and architecture. but the bauhaus doctrine as a whole never took root again after the destruction of the bauhaus by the nazis. i am saying something about the bauhaus at this conference because we are starting a new institution – a continuation of the bauhaus – for which walter gropius has given me his full support. it is the so-called hochschule für gestaltung at ulm (the translation of the name may be 'college of design'). we are just starting with the buildings which will be finished in spring 1954. on 1 august the first group of students will arrive – some students are already collaborating in our construction office. but it is not only on account of the actuality of these facts that i am speaking about this project. it is also for the reason that we are very grateful to the american people and their authorities for the great help they have given us for our project. in the first place, above all, mr john j mccloy and his consultants gave us their support and took on responsibility for helping us to realise our plans.

this is the story: during the war, there were a few students in munich fighting against the nazi regime and for freedom. they prepared a student rebellion against the regime. they were captured and executed by the nazis. they were six and among them a brother and sister – the scholls – who were the important leaders. after the war, the father of these two became mayor of the town of ulm. ulm is a place of 100,000 inhabitants together with its environs, a town with a good industry and the highest church tower in the world. in the middle ages, a population of about 9,000 people built this dome for 20,000 people. ulm not only has the highest tower, but a man was born there who is today known for his high ideals, as a leading figure in science and morality – the great philosopher and scientist albert einstein. in ulm after the war, the scholls' sister, inge scholl, founded an evening school for adult education because she said 'all political excesses originate from ignorance and stupidity: if i can help to educate people, political sense will become better'. so she worked in her school with a very good programme for adult education. the best-known people of germany and foreign countries gave lectures at her school. it was in 1948 that i went through ulm for the first time and got in contact with this school and the leading people of the community … since then, i have always been in good contact with these people. it is now four years since i received a letter from ulm, containing a programme for a new school with more social and political accents and the invitation to collaborate as consultant and architect. i learned that mr mccloy had offered inge scholl his support for her activities in ulm.

at this time, inge scholl founded the 'geschwister-scholl-stiftung' as the organisation undertaking the new school project. my contact with the whole planning of the school became more and more close, so that the foundation asked me if I would accept the position of the rector of the school and the head of the architectural faculty. long before this, we founded a committee of trustees in which men like van de velde and gropius are together with men of science and humanities.

now i had the chance to realise the pedagogical idea i had always been talking about. after long negotiations, we got a promise from mr mccloy that, if we could collect a matching sum as high as the american contribution, we would receive the money for building and equipping the school. in working this out, over the two years inge scholl worked like sisyphus. if we finally came to a result, it was on account of the prestige of the brother and sister scholl and the generous gesture of mr mccloy who, together with mrs mccloy, last year brought the cheque to ulm just before leaving germany. so we had taken a good step toward the realisation. i will not tell you how many further steps had to be taken until the date i mentioned, and how many things had to be settled with the german authorities regarding intrigues from several sides. just these days now, we are starting with the buildings and in five weeks our first courses will begin. most of our teachers are friends of mine, old and young, and come from several countries. we are a team. i am telling you all this as a demonstration of the theme: why aren't there more schools of the bauhaus type? and i will give you the key to the answer: in ulm, there are several chances coming together: a leading group of young idealists, the will to resist the tendencies of nazism as symbolised by the brother and sister scholl, the open hand of the US high commissioner john mccloy and his consultants, a good climate at the community of ulm, prepared by the *volkshochschule*, well-meaning town and local government authorities, some interest from industry in getting new models for production and, last but not least, a team willing to teach under conditions which are perhaps not the best from an economic point of view, but as compensation they have a certain independence. i must underline that our school is an independent one, and that government and community only give us a certain amount of support. i could tell you now what we will be doing in this school, but i hope you will certainly see results in a short time, and results are always much more significant than promising programmes. in short, we are educating creative people to be able to do useful things for everyday life. that's all my information about ulm. on this occasion, i wish to express our deep gratitude to your nation for your important support of our project. i am happy in giving my thanks to you here, at the aspen design conference, the first audience i am meeting in the states, coming here for the first time.

let's now go back to the notion of 'design'. before turning to the history of the ulm school, i spoke about morality and responsibility in design. for me the moral background for design comes first. the designer is responsible for his work. and that is just what i want to underline: a designer must be a top-notch artist, not second rate. design is a responsible work in getting the culture of our time. in this sense art, as pure art, is the forerunner of everyday design. but from the cultural point of view, design is as important as art because design goes into mass production for everyday consumption. here business can help, the education of the consumer can help. but, as stated before, unfortunately business often goes the wrong way, and is interested in sleek design rather than really good design. a lot of today's design is for waste, it is done only for business and not for cultural reasons.

and here we come to the notion of 'decoration'. decoration is something extra, an addition. it is not primarily useful. personally i am against decoration. i do not like it either in the old or in the modern sense, but in the modern sense, this play with symbols – like squares and the use of all of these pure forms in design, typography and decoration – is a nonsense. most of the streamlined goods, decorated with snaky lines and the funniest lineaments, without any other function than to bluff the uneducated customer, go against every moral sense. designers are responsible for these things. they must have the power to resist such demands of ignorant clients.

here i must add a few words about the living conditions and independence of the designer. a word to the students first, because they will be responsible in the future. if you are studying, you think perhaps of getting a good job one day. this is an illusion. if you are an independently working designer, your conditions will not be much better than those of so-called free artists. you will always be dependent on economic facts. the only way you can make it is to work more or less in teams; at the same time you must be able to change your living conditions and be happy under every condition. but always you must be free to say 'no'. you have to exchange security for adventure, you must be able to drive for many years the best car in the world and go by foot tomorrow. with this risk you buy your freedom and your existence as a moral human being. under these conditions you will become a good designer.

i will show you an example of good design and give a critique: here i have a parker pen. it is the cheap model. i do not have this cheap model because it is cheap, but because it is a better design. there exists a parker 51, with a silly decoration in the form of a plume on its clip. why? certainly not for reasons of function. my cheap one is absolutely perfect in the construction of the clip, but the clip of the expensive one is for decoration only, really worthless. i am asking, would the designer of the parker go around as a beggar if he refused to make such a bad design and said: i am doing one model, you can produce it for different prices, one with gold, the other with steel. if you are looking at the parker … you see that it is a useful instrument and has many well-designed characteristics: i will speak only about the name parker and the cap. most of the products are completely destroyed by the imprinting of the name of the producer or his trademark. i mention two extreme cases, first dunhill. if you look at a dunhill pipe you will only see a white point, marking 'i am by dunhill'. then a german firm is producing a series of new models in stainless steel – a knife, fork and spoon. the models are done well, but the nice form is spoiled by inscriptions and marks. not so the parker pen: the name is engraved in the best possible manner on the cap. but why did the designer do two models of cap – a really good one and a bad one?

on the examples of the pens, i was showing you the typical result for decoration, and moving further down the alphabet i come now to 'form'. i mention this for two reasons: first, because form is the result of any design, secondly, i wrote a book entitled 'form'. the book is written in german, french and english, in simultaneous text. there you will find some remarks that i cannot speak about today. i do not have enough time to repeat all i have written there and in another book, 'idea', in which is printed a longer essay of mine talking about 'beauty as result of function, and beauty as function'. these two books are the only ones that i have written in english about problems of design. i have mentioned this for your information only and also for underlining that communication could find easier outlets than conferences.

it would take a lot of time to speak about form today, and we could hardly speak about it without mentioning the notion of 'function'. so i will explain only my own point of view on this question of the relation of form and function. one of the really great architects said some time ago: form does not follow function. i do not agree with him. form must follow function; without function, form cannot exist. but i must add that function alone is no argument for a good form. it would never be good to make form *against* function. one cannot exist without the other. the important question is only how to make a good form for a determined function. and this we cannot explain, inasmuch as it is an act of creation – some are able to create, others not, some do it better, some not so good. the ability to create cannot be learned, the only thing we can learn is one more step, following the alphabet: 'm' for morality and its sister, modesty.

i believe this is perhaps the most important of all the things i wish to tell you. by 'morality' i understand the 'action of the individual against temptations of the society, action of the individual in the sense of common interest and common health'. this means that for every action of an individual, this individual is personally responsible. so every action from one individual to another, or against society, must have a moral background. take the example of art. do you think that we all often understand that the notion of 'art' is coming out of a moral background? never. the bigger part of art ranks somewhere between harmless self-deception and a very clear swindle against the public. most of this so-called art comes out of vanity, or often is only bluff. but real art can only grow on a moral background and with a sense of responsibility. but how is it with the moral background for culture and design? culture without a moral background is decadence. design without a moral background is a crime against society. bad design turns the environment of human life into an ugly one, it infiltrates ugly things into the subconscious of men, it makes life a nonsense since life only has sense at a high level of culture, in a well-ordered and harmonious environment. this is why we are working. it is about morality.

and now 'modesty': like morality, modesty is one of the most important attitudes of human existence. modesty is very close to morality and grows out of it. modesty in the field of art does not mean mediocrity. on the contrary, modesty in art and design means 'to do a work only with the absolute tendency to do something as well as possible'. for the plastic arts it means to do a work as an objective realisation of an objective idea, without any self-expression, so that one day everybody can understand the signification of this objective and universal language. only in this way do works of art grow to new symbols and messages in the old and magic sense of art. in this way, art will become of much bigger interest in a time of plenty, which certainly is coming. art and design will then become a wide field of activity, as art will really be one of the creative parts of life, namely the highest expression of the human mind. and design will be more important for its sole purpose: it will no longer serve the interests of sales and competition, but will bring harmony to our environment.

if all of us – designers and producers, artists and critics – were to work with the same honesty and the same modesty, we could certainly change our nervous and hasty life. if designers were only to do honest and modest design and resist other demands, good design would be found more often and still improve in quality. and *this* better design will finally pay off – perhaps not in money, but in a harmonious life.

THE BASIS AND AIM OF AESTHETICS IN THE MACHINE AGE (1953)

Madam Chairwoman, Ladies and Gentlemen,

I'd like to begin by thanking the Institut d'esthétique industrielle, and especially Mr Vienot, for organising this conference.

I bring you greetings from the central committee of the Swiss Werkbund, an association that for 40 years has had as its aim the promotion of pure utilitarian form.

I have a few reservations about the purpose of this conference, since in my experience agendas that are loaded with too many unresolved issues – ie, that attempt to tackle more than a single, precisely formulated theme – tend not to produce results. But we'll see whether my concerns turn out to be well founded, or whether I'm mistaken.

The conference is based around the term 'esthétique industrielle' (industrial aesthetics). I don't want to talk about this term today. For a variety of reasons I don't recognise it; I hold it for false. The reasons for this are given in my book *form*.

This conference is also assembled under a sign (the conference logo) that I would describe as pretty much embodying the idea that 'decoration does not deceive' or even, as one of the speakers put it yesterday, 'decoration is simultaneously a symbol'. I ask you to take a closer look at this 'symbol', that you're all wearing on your lapels: you'll see a powerful 'I' with a little snake twined around it, identifiable as the 'e' of this pairing. I'll not go into whether this kind of 'symbolism' was intentional or not – the powerful 'I' for industry, with the entwined 'e' for 'esthétique' – but will simply note that this sign now exists in this form, as the logo of this conference.

So we're trying to operate under this 'symbol' indicating that aesthetics adorns industry. While some people here may proceed on this basis without further thought, I can hardly believe this would be the starting point for all participants in the conference. This 'symbol' certainly doesn't work for those who are here as delegates from ideological associations such as the Swiss or the German Werkbunds. And, speaking just for myself and as a delegate of the central committee of the Swiss Werkbund, I have to tell you that our efforts are increasingly directed towards people's needs, rather than the demands of industry. You can see here a fundamental difference in outlook, and we could easily devote a hard week of exhaustive debate to clarifying its consequences. In spite of this, we all hope to find a common working basis for this conference, and to take new knowledge back home with us.

I've made a few notes and beg your pardon for expressing myself in a kind of simplified French, like a 10-year-old. Perhaps, though, the Anglo-Saxons will find me easier to understand than some of the earlier speakers, and we'll be able to do without a translator.

For a long time moralists and socialists have called for pure utilitarian form. By this they understand forms that are beautiful and practical, for all objects. In this context I would like to mention above all the great pioneer Henry van de Velde, who coined the term 'rational beauty'.

The problem of beauty and practicality is widely recognised, not only in the sphere of production but also among consumers. Yet we still cannot say that the moralists' and pioneers' demands have become reality today.

If we ask ourselves why there is still this discrepancy between real needs and production, the answer is clear: every single manufacturer's understanding of the term 'beautiful' is essentially different. One lot may understand the exact opposite from the other, the same applies to consumers, and so we can assume that the same differences of conception prevail among those who are involved in the aesthetics, drafting and design of use-objects.

And this is where the difficulties begin: the term 'beautiful' means something different to everyone.

'Beauty' is therefore too uncertain an argument to use as the starting point for a discussion of 'industrial form-giving'.

'Industrial form-giving' is the name people have given to the application of aesthetic concerns to industrial production. As I've already stated, I do not believe in this kind of 'industrial form-giving'; it's a juxtaposition of terms that in my view is nonsensical. I think what we're talking about is not so much an 'industrial aesthetic' or form-giving, as an aesthetic or approach that is not only determined by but also serves industry or, more exactly, serves to influence industrial products.

We all know why this problem has assumed such great importance: it's because the output of mass production has to conform to the expectations of large numbers of consumers. The basis of such an 'industrial aesthetic' is not the pure use-form, or rational beauty: the basis is always manufacture for an anonymous consuming public – that is, for a mass of buyers whose aesthetic sensibilities may not be taken into account.

Thus pure beauty, pure form, are excluded from everyday life and carve out a solitary existence in the so-called liberal arts. They emerge from this isolation only late in life, when they are drawn, almost ineluctably, into the storage facilities for the past, into museums. But the real function of these artworks, at the time of their creation, ought not to be overlooked. The most audacious works of contemporary art act both conceptually and formally as standards for everyday goods and industrial objects. Nonetheless, 'taste' remains in effect, constantly dictating the output of mass production. So until we find a way around this ill-defined starting point, any discussion will always be complicated by this indeterminate factor.

After years of experience in a variety of different fields I've now reached the point where I believe it's possible to bypass the discussion about what is beautiful or ugly, pure form or pure use-form. It's five years now since I made a presentation at the 1948 conference of the Swiss Werkbund on 'beauty from function and as function' [see pp. 32–41]. What I then held to be true – the idea that beauty plays a very important role – I no longer believe to the same extent, which brings me to the questions that I'd like to put to you.

It appears self-evident that the purpose of this huge variety of machine-made objects should be to serve people. They have to fulfil a totality of functions, with their qualities being assessed according to the principles of solidity, use value, beauty, affordability. We will use these various principles and qualities as a lens through which to examine the objects.

'Solidity' is purely a manufacturing problem. It is possible to manufacture all kinds of products with all kinds of life-span. This relates to the purpose of the object, whether it's intended for long-term or limited use. Here's an example: a paper napkin versus a linen napkin. In this case the problem of the use-value is clear. But let's take another example: an iron. It's possible to make irons that are virtually indestructible. But it's also possible to make them so that they have to be thrown away after a while, not because their form has become obsolete, but because they are deliberately not made solid enough. Theoretically it's possible to make an iron equipped with all the twentieth-century gizmos – the cream of the crop, incorporating every possible innovation, an iron that would last forever. But we rarely come across an object that has been produced in this way, because it's not in the manufacturer's interests. For what would he produce if there were no need for new irons in the future? This means that economic factors determine how solid an iron can be. The manufacturer prefers selling large quantities at a low price to selling only a few expensive items. For he hopes that new models of iron can be continually produced and sold.

The 'use-value' is the next argument. The example of the napkin seems to be clear, that of the iron already more complicated. We know that all kinds of iron are in use. But some are more practical than others, some are easier to handle, others get better results, or are less demanding to use. Why, then, does nobody make an iron that combines all of the good qualities? Today this is not so much a question of manufacture as a question of design – and mostly the bad design of the so-called 'industrial designer'. The majority of irons, even the latest models, have highly questionable forms that mostly conceal technical imperfections; this is precisely what we have to thank the 'designer' for. So we see an aesthetic and moral problem here, where we least expected it.

With the example of the napkin, which at first seemed so straightforward, we encounter more problems. Paper can be used to make any number of variations, from an imitation lace doily to an ingenious paper structure. Likewise the linen fabric opens up a wide array of weaving techniques. Here, 'taste' is usually the determinant of 'beauty' and, by extension, 'practicality'.

With the iron the problems of beauty are much more complicated, because the so-called 'artistic vision' is constrained by a host of technical details and requirements. So besides beauty there are other problems that stand in the foreground: the questions of production and function.

Yet in contrast to the other elements 'beauty' arises not of itself but is to a certain extent derived out of a close observance of the remaining factors of production. Beauty can indeed be the self-evident outcome of the unity of all functions, but it can also be added artificially, in the absence of a real functional need for it, so long as one does not treat the commercial arguments as similarly indispensable.

Here we confront the difficulty of 'industrial design' or 'formgiving'. A dividing line splits this whole field into two different areas with different approaches: on one side you have contrived decoration, on the other true design. On one side are decorators, on the other designers.

It is regrettable that the majority of industrialists, when they need someone to advise them on matters of form, usually turn to a decorator rather than a true designer. This is a moment when true designers ought to be getting involved in production, for there is a danger that today's superficial ornamentation will simply give way to a new decorative style. This is a moment when manufacturers and designers have to shoulder an equal responsibility.

I believe there is no need here to examine why the machine age, our age, has failed to fully realise the hopes invested in it in the early days of industrialisation. I'm just making this observation as a way of broaching, not so much the aesthetic questions this raises, as the social consequences.

Here we encounter a mass of unresolved problems; so if we speak of the basis and aim of aesthetics in the machine age, it always has to be in relation to these unresolved social issues. Even if we're concerned with other things at the moment, namely with the 'aesthetics' that are a specific underlying theme of this conference, we should not forget that aesthetics must never serve as decoration, as a facade for covering up those things that even today, despite numerous reforms, still don't function to our complete satisfaction.

If we consider the question of aesthetics from an ideal viewpoint, then the aesthetic appearance is simultaneously the correct appearance, the expression of what is right. What we're searching for is therefore not so much an indefinable aesthetic expression as a true and correct solution to a given task. It is for this reason alone that I speak here of the 'basis and aim of aesthetics in the machine age'.

The basis of any aesthetic has to be above all function. This is perhaps a somewhat general term; what I mean is that an exemplary object should fulfil its purpose under all conditions – practical, as well as social. In other words it should fulfil, completely and under all conditions, the function for which it was created. This means, for example, that if a typewriter is to completely fulfil its function as a typewriter it must be simultaneously pleasing to look at, no bigger than is absolutely required, easy to maintain and finally value for money, ie worth the financial outlay. Whether it is made by hand or machine – whether it's 'hand-crafted' or 'industrial' – is of no concern to us here.

For that is a purely economic question, which has always to be assessed in relation to the specific category of goods.

What we consider to be the necessary prerequisites for the typewriter apply equally to any other object. The difference here is not so much between objects, as between categories, as we can see if we take two examples that seem to be miles apart – a sculpture and a plane. What we demand from the plane as its primary function is technical performance, that is the capacity to transport a set load from one place to another in the shortest possible time, and under specific economic conditions. The sculpture, on the other hand, has to fulfil a purely spiritual function, find a formal expression for it. Between these two extremes lies an expansive field composed of an infinite variety of objects; in some of these the external appearance plays an important role, in others it is considered unimportant. But in all cases a sum of functions has to be fulfilled. So it is always paramount to analyse these functions as precisely as possible and define each one individually. This is the task and the difficulty of form-giving. It is therefore not so much the question of aesthetics as the analysis of functions that is the remit of the true designer.

With aesthetics, we have observed that taste does not offer sufficient certainty. Nor are the quality of the material or the technical execution in themselves enough. It's only the 'function of the whole' that can form a valid basis for operation. We might therefore ask: how, then, do we come to a form? And in light of the preceding argument we should note: the form is not the basis of the things, but a result; it is the expression, the bringing together of the various functions, to which the quality of unity adheres. We then perceive this unity of all functions as a valid, typical form, as *gestalt*.

By this I do not mean either the simple, stylised form, or the beautiful form, but rather the organic form.

Picture the various aggregated functions of a car and you can see an almost accidental combination of mechanistic, formal and functional intentions, all aimed at fulfilling the most varied requirements. From this example we can understand why it was not so easy to progress from the four-wheeled coach to a more or less serviceable car. And yet today's car, even after 50 years of development, is not yet a unified construction, not yet a 'unity of functions'.

The same goes for building. Here too the functions are often so vague and ill defined that it's not surprising if the results represent not so much the 'unity of functions' as the architect's desire for self-expression. With regard to this I'd like to point out the real danger of this kind of personal expression becoming a substitute for a clear definition of functions, preventing the 'unity of all functions' from developing into a neutral, organic and typical form. It is this neutral, typical organic form that I take as my ideal.

You might ask, 'why this neutral form?' My answer is that these neutral, functional forms are the most beautiful ones; because they are exempt from the vagaries of fashion they are more enduring and in this way they become characteristic of the type of object. It is this character of the object, its purpose, that I'd like to see expressed, rather than the personality of the designer, with his more or less perishable plays on form.

Perhaps you will then ask, 'but what are we, as designers of form, meant to do with such a restrictive programme? Isn't this more the territory of technicians and engineers? Where is the art in such a programme? Where are the creative possibilities?' My response is that when it comes to creating something, to designing, the prerequisite is a certain degree of artistic maturity. I even believe that it is necessary for this very field of 'art' to create not just so-called free art, but also objects for daily use. I am convinced that each thing made by a true artist is a work of art, even when the artist is quite clearly working in a fully objective manner, with no ambitions of 'self-expression'. Finally – and forgive my saying so – it's only the artist who is truly creative. If you come across engineers that you admire on account of their creative achievements, then they are the artists among engineers. It is the creative side of the engineer that speaks to us. If we now connect the concept of the artistic, as described above, with objective, analytical and synthetic work, then we have defined the basis for the work of the designer, whose goal it should be to bind the unity of all functions into an optimally usable form. In this way we arrive at the answer to the question about the 'basis and aim of aesthetics in the machine age'.

I believe I have adequately defined the aim of production as the fulfilling of people's needs. If we take this aim as the basis of every design, does it then become identical with the purpose and aim of aesthetics? Not quite. For on a larger scale, the real purpose behind the influence of aesthetics on production is not only to 'fulfil people's needs' but to give life in its totality a more harmonious, more beautiful and more joyful basis – to give it meaning.

If we accept that the technology of the machine age has improved our living conditions, we should not allow the price we generally pay for this improvement – increased levels of stress – to negate the advantages of 'technical progress'. When we speak of the aim of a contemporary aesthetic, we know what goal to aim for. The way to achieving it, however, is not so easy to define.

Here we confront a typical phenomenon of the machine age, which unfortunately also provides ammunition for all the enemies of industrialisation: mechanisation doesn't function for life, but is an end in itself. However, we maintain that we are only at the beginning of a process of industrialisation; our knowledge and capabilities are still somewhat rudimentary. Our time is characterised as the machine age. But it is not yet the time of machines that serve people. We believe in the power of the machine, but we do not yet have the kind of culture that one would expect to support this technical development. We have only some small indications of this, so feeble that the pessimists cannot be convincingly refuted. True, machines are productive, the atomic age is dawning. But this is profiting only a few, rather than being in the service of all, rather than working for people's real needs, for their well-being.

I do not want – either here or elsewhere – to connect this assertion with superannuated socialist claims; I'm merely emphasising that we have to recognise the need to get ourselves out of our current situation, and then find the means and ways to do this, if there is to be any point at all to this whole 'technological progress'. We must make a transition from the machine age to the age of humanism – a humanism in the best sense of the word, a humanism in which people, their needs and their desires, determine trade and production; in other words, the machine age must become the age of people who are served by machines, liberated by them, rather than enslaved by them as they are today.

But how do we get there? Can artists and aestheticians help to build this future world? Of course they can. Artists represent the vision of the future, their duty is to direct the common interest towards this goal. But what can artists and those concerned with aesthetics do right now? There are unlimited possibilities of production; they have to be exploited in a comprehensive way. A large number of needs can be fulfilled, and new ones are constantly arising. Satisfying these needs calls for a high standard of production. It requires artists to take on the moral responsibility for ensuring that the totality of functions is grasped and formed in its entirety, as the basis of production. Through this, the artist will be in a position to influence the culture of tomorrow.

But the artist has a responsibility for today's culture too. He must make a stand, get involved in production that serves others. But we see a great danger here: we see designers beginning to apply decoration to industrial products before they can be certain they've established the required totality of functions. These 'artists' are responsible for the decline of culture. They are responsible for the fact that a large number of use-objects are 'embellished' without regard for their character or purpose, decorated with modernistic features or encased in an aerodynamic shell. In short, they are responsible for all the nonsense that we encounter today. What they're doing is perhaps understandable from a marketing point of view, but in relation to the development of our culture, the culture of humanism, it is reprehensible.

I'll therefore close with the following statements that sum up my position.

1. The task of the artist is not to express himself and his feelings in a subjective way; it is to create harmonious objects that will serve people.

2. Artists have to grapple with the problems of serial production; it's part of their responsibility for human culture.

3. The basis of all production should be to fulfil, as a unity, the totality of all functions, including the aesthetic functions of an object.

4. The aim of all production should be to satisfy people's needs and desire for a harmonious life.

CONTINUITY AND CHANGE (1953)

In tackling this theme we must first of all consider what
we understand by the two terms, 'continuity' and 'change'.

Continuity refers to that which persists, continues
to exist, always in the same form, with the same value.
Change is the opposite of continuity. It is that which
mutates, albeit within certain limits. It doesn't refer to the
kind of instant transformation, with no intermediate steps,
that you get in fairy-tales for example, when a frog morphs
into a prince.

If, however, we want to investigate these terms more
closely, we need to find a measure that can be applied
both to the constant and the mutable. If we were to use the
measure of geological time, the only constant connecting
these two terms would be a formula to the effect that the
energy mass always remains the same.

By energy mass, I do not mean the form in which
the energy is materialised, but simply the amount of
energy. For while the amount of energy remains constant,
it appears in a variety of forms that are subject to continual
change. From this one might conclude that continuity is
not to be found in materials, but only in ideas, and perhaps
only then in an idea that has remained unaltered with the
passage of time. To avoid any possible misunderstanding,
I'd like here to equate idea with energy.

If we now look at what is happening today, we see a
world being transformed. If we could replay the events on
earth in some kind of time-lapse motion, we'd witness, over
the millennia, a change of tremendous proportions. The
course of history would then be measured in terms of the
speed of light.

From this example you can see that the concepts
of continuity and change are both relative. This means we

have to ask ourselves: what are the conditions framing this continuity and this change? Even when we limit the terms of our investigation to our own life-spans, we can see that we use a variety of measures – minutes, hours, days, weeks, months, years, decades – to mark the passage of time and gauge continuity and change.

From this perspective it's easy to succumb to the temptation to view nothing as constant and everything as mutable (or, conversely, depending on the time-span under review, everything as constant and nothing as mutable). It's therefore time that serves as a measure, it's the duration that counts.

In this context we find continuity in things where change is not immediately obvious. And change in things where the transformation is quite apparent.

In addition, with objects, we relate continuity and change to the life-span of the thing itself, in other words we judge a chair, for example, not only in terms of its individual qualities but also as a representation of a type – chairs as a whole over a longer time-span. We then see within an individual object elements not only of continuity but also of change.

If we're addressing this topic today, it's mainly because we want to be clear about our relation to so-called continuity and so-called change. We want to know what function continuity has, what function change has. And we want to know how to respond to them.

Since this is a question not just of artistic concern but of greater social interest, we need to recognise that both continuity and change are essential, indeed inseparable components of the artistic. And more than this: both are essential foundations of society.

The question is therefore: to what end continuity, to what end change? Or, more specifically, what should be constant, what should change?

Taking as our starting point people's needs, it's evident that these vary from place to place. Nevertheless there are certain basic things that all people need – forks, knives, spoons, plates, cups, chairs, tables, beds and other

everyday objects of this kind. There are regional variations
in use. So, for example, in China and Japan they don't
use forks but chopsticks. Chairs also take on different
forms depending on where and how they're being used.
But within a region there is little variation in an object's
perceived purpose. Given this stability of purpose and use,
one would expect a certain continuity. But just look at our
cutlery and the way it has developed! It's clear that it has
undergone a huge number of changes, and it's hard to find
a single spoon whose form is untouched by contemporary
styling, never mind one defined solely by its distinct
(though versatile) use. So we have external, artificial stylistic
changes exerting an influence over the continuity of the
perceived purpose, thereby regulating the continuity of the
form. I'm not sure whether the desire to have a spoon for
all times – which always looks the same because it's always
used the same way – should be put down to a striving for
perfection, or a striving for freedom, or a striving for
absolutism. Or whether the spoon is continually tinkered
with out of some irrepressible instinct for play or desire
for variation.

I do, however, believe that the spoon is continually
changing because we haven't yet found its true form –
the form that corresponds to all its different functions. This
form depends less on some stroke of creative inspiration
than it does on its purpose, which has first to be defined
and then comprehensively tested. From this we get a form
that is provisional at first, and requires patient development to become what we call *gestalt*. *Gestalt* in this sense
is more than form: it embraces that which is valid, constant.
I'd like to call this kind of change 'organic development',
in that it arises out of the givens of function, with the
proviso that when the purpose changes the *gestalt* does too.

Taking this route will ultimately lead us to look for
– and find – the *gestalt* of all the things around us. Styles
will effectively disappear; it will no longer be a case of *one*
style simply being replaced by *another*, giving way to a new
idea of form. One may recall previous misguided efforts
to reduce everything to its so-called 'primary form' – to

spheres, cones, cylinders, etc. The intention was to go beyond style, but all that actually happened was that a new style was substituted for an old one. That kind of 'purification' of formal vocabulary is not what I'm recommending here. What I advocate instead is a search for the constant, a search for the valid *gestalt*. *Gestalt*, in this sense, is distinguished by its essential simplicity – not an artificial simplification, not stylisation, but simple and correct function.

And also beauty – not an artificially applied beauty, but a self-evident beauty. Objects of this kind presuppose a modesty on the part of the designer. Any eruptions of 'self-expression' (as the Anglo-Saxons so beautifully put it) would be out of place here, for the decisive factor is not the expression of the designer but the expression of the object, which has to neutrally fulfil its purpose. But being 'without style' is not the same as being characterless. Such objects in fact have a very distinctive character. They just don't have 'style', as one woman defined it when instructing Adolf Loos on the subject – she said that the same emblem should be applied to all objects and all pieces of furniture. In the example Loos related this was a lion's head in the so-called arts and crafts style. Later this kind of emblem evolved into the steel pipe or the spherical lamp. And later still into the pair of decorative lines that are to be found on most American use-objects today. Even the really pale wood that is currently being used for all sorts of pieces of furniture derives from a similar spirit – from an impulse towards external uniformity – that has nothing to do with the *gestalt* of the things.

If we want to try to give things their own form today, if we want *gestalt*, then we cannot operate according to the principles that have been in use up to now. We must turn towards new methods instead. These methods are to be found in morphology, in the study of *gestalt*. The founders of morphology, principally Goethe and Roux, used scientific methods in an attempt to understand the laws that structure the formation of organisms, that is, the connections between their functions as well as the changes in function. Theirs was an analytical investigation, aimed at defining an applicable theory of formation. Morphology is still mostly approached in this analytical/comparative manner, that is, as a comparative investigation of the structure and functioning of organisms and the ways in which they change.

But what we need today is a synthetic, creative morphology, a creative theory of form. Just as we can draw on existing work in our own investigations, so we can anticipate future needs based on our present levels of knowledge.

The things created by man are certainly of a different order than plants or animals, which are the result of a long, self-correcting series of developments, a metamorphosis. With this in mind, we could also use the theory of form to demonstrate that all things are subject to change, including living organisms, which are continually seeking to adapt to new conditions.

Applying morphology to a thing means considering the connections between all its elements and all its functions, its technical properties and ultimately also its appearance. No one element should dominate – instead, all of them need to stand in harmonious agreement. With this, we leave the realm of applied arts far behind and enter uncharted territory.

You may ask: but where does this leave continuity? And I can only respond: there's continuity in our purpose. However our purpose is also to see – and to see clearly. We are not working for the sake of machines, for some impersonal, superordinate entity such as 'industry' or 'state' or 'community'. We're working for the wellbeing of every person, every individual, as part of a community. We're trying to develop things that can serve everyone equally, make their lives better, more beautiful, and allow them to develop their potential more freely. This purpose, this new humanism, is what I'd like to see as continuity.

It's to this end that we're working to create a relative continuity in things, to this end that we're always calling for quality. At first this was technical quality – things that are well made and therefore good value, things that last, because we see no reason to always be changing them. Then formal quality can be characterised as the sum of all factors that are taken into account in the design and that are reflected in – and indeed shape – the form as a whole. Formal quality is the mark of an object that is functional in all respects.

But where does this leave imagination and art? I believe this is a valid question, as we need to find a way out of this dilemma in which we find ourselves (and have found ourselves for decades): art *or* daily life, art *or* function.

It might at first seem that you don't need to collaborate with artists to define a morphological basis for formal qualities. It might seem that an engineer would be in a position to calculate and construct everything. One Swiss engineer speaking at a recent conference in Darmstadt certainly seemed to think so. He related how he'd been asked whether a gifted young man should become an architect. And he replied, 'if he's gifted, then let him become an architect. If he's very gifted, then he should be an engineer.' Cue heavy applause from his audience. One can see this story as an indication of the depths to which our expectations of art, including architecture, have sunk. But I don't believe this is the right attitude, or that the right solution can be found this way. Indeed I believe that when an engineer makes something that's good in every respect, it's because the artist in him is shining through. But it shows a complete misunderstanding of the role of the architect and the artist in society to imagine that they could be replaced by a gifted engineer. At least not the kind of engineer who comes out of today's schools, with today's views. It seems to me that those who are truly gifted should become not just engineers, but truly creative designers of everyday objects. For I believe that in the current climate of specialisation people with artistic skills are needed to bring together the different fields. Their ability to do so depends largely on their education. And here I'm in agreement with the engineer who spoke at Darmstadt: better a gifted engineer than a middling architect or so-called artist. And better a knowledgeable engineer than an untutored artist.

And now I'd like to come back to the real theme. As I've said, continuity is our goal – our duty to people, the new humanism. Thus broadly defined, this goal, if it's taken seriously, is not subject to change. But the paths that lead to it are certainly very varied. There are many possible routes. As a small but typical example, I'd like to refer once again to the spoon and point out that, even given the most careful morphological research, its formal quality can turn out to be quite variable. Not everything that makes up form can be reviewed and quantified, so different variants can result – with spoons, just as with songbirds in nature – even if these differences are visually subtle and their purpose, their function, is difficult to define in relation to either their form or use. We therefore see that the same function can take on several different forms even without the input of artificial or artistic devices. So it's redundant to insist, on top of this, that we should give the alleged imagination free rein to turn the simple function of a spoon into an artwork – or a sorry excuse.

By itself, the manufacturing process can generate different forms of a spoon. These forms are not shaped morphologically, but are determined by production techniques. So when we go against our better judgement and change the form of a spoon for technical reasons – the sort of thing that happens all the time in industry – we are subordinating the spoon's meaning and purpose to production methods, and abandoning part of the postulate which maintains that a spoon ought to be at the service of people – not machines. What emerges from such an approach is an inferior but possibly cheaper spoon or, in the best-case scenario, a spoon of average quality and utility. But under no circumstances do you get a spoon that is morphologically correct and displays the formal quality we are calling for. From this example of a typical, though demanding, object like a spoon you can see that design issues are very closely related to production processes, and that up to now technology has been unable (or more often unwilling) to tackle those things for which rationally there is only one production method – one that proceeds according to our best judgement.

On the other hand, technology has not yet advanced to the stage where it's possible to manufacture anything we desire. This has a bearing on the programme I've sketched out above. Until we're able to produce a constant form in an economically viable way we can hardly avoid all the deviations from this constant, all the deficiencies of function that apparently need to be offset with meaningless things such as decoration and attention-grabbing design.

I've sketched out the influence of technical factors from the perspective of industry. Handcrafts are more flexible in this respect, as – putting aside the cost – craftsmen can produce individual works that achieve a perfect agreement between material and form. This gives one-off manufacture a distinct advantage, provided we don't take the economics into account. But often it is precisely this financial aspect – the risk for investors – that poses the biggest obstacle to the industrial production of an object. The manufacturing process is only one side of the equation. The other side is the material, which influences the character of the spoon. We have access to the most varied materials, each with their own advantages and disadvantages: wood, porcelain, silver, zinc, chrome, plastics, to name just a few. Each has a different weight and surface texture, which by itself leads to different forms. A light spoon has different formal qualities than a heavy one. Hence, in the absence of agreement on a single material that is suitable for all spoons, each material, as a consequence of its specific properties, will inevitably yield a different end product. All of these can be morphologically correct – in theory at least. The variants are not arbitrary, but arise solely out of the properties of the material: they are given by nature and have nothing at all to do with capricious plays of form.

You will perhaps ask again why we need artists at all if the creativity of the individual is going to be so constrained that the difference between maker and artist is erased. If you're one of those gifted individuals who can't get excited at the prospect of things that endure for a long time, I'd like to point you towards those areas that live by change – and rapid change, not slow evolution.

If I have placed such an emphasis on relative continuity, on slow morphological development, it's not because I consider this the only possible approach to ordering life. But I do believe that these standard objects can to a certain extent provide the foundation for making our lives easier. If someone wants to go further than this in pursuing their individual goals, and has the necessary means to do so, then they have any number of options open to them.

For example in fashion, where creative people can give a suit or a coat a perfect fit and a harmonious line – a line that changes with every year, to our continual surprise and delight. Changes in fashion always mirror changing times, either in micro-form or, just as often, in a magnified way. How connected they are with time and place can once again be demonstrated by referring to an example given by that tireless critic Adolf Loos, the example of the top hat. The top hat used to be considered a symbol of timeless elegance. (You don't necessarily have to agree, of course.) But Loos observed that if 20 top hats from the past 100 years were displayed together, and a top-hat wearer was asked to pick one out, he would invariably choose the latest model. But how do Loos's top hats concern us? They are an example of a standard that, while being a standard, is also a fashion, and thus subject to change.

We don't want to rule out this kind of fashion. It has a part to play in contemporary life, just as history does: neither can be ignored, and both are a potential source of inspiration.

But we must always be clear about one thing: as much as fashion may bring us pleasure, as much as we revere the historical, we should never forget that both of these things – the fashionable (as the thing which changes the most) as well as the historical (which became historical because everything changed) – only have real meaning when they're related to our constant goal, namely, the idea of serving man. That is why we need those standard objects which will create the basis for a higher standard of living – and to which changes in fashion can then be an enjoyable addition.

FORM, FUNCTION, BEAUTY = GESTALT

If I've been speaking to you about these standard objects, which currently lack good form, and about ways to go about making them, it is because these are precisely the things that surround us every day and that cumulatively form our environment. If these objects are created in the way I've just described, they will become components of our culture – consumer goods will become cultural goods. This is the route by which art can leave its ivory tower and return to life – no longer as a substitute for life, but as an integral, supporting part of it.

GOOD FORMAL DESIGN (1953)

Ladies and Gentlemen,

It is a great honour to be permitted to speak to you in Ulm [at a meeting of your association, the Neue Gemeinschaft für Wohnkultur (WK)]. But a wholly involuntary one. In a sense, I am *compelled* to speak here as a corollary of my local duties.

Since I don't like speaking, yet am obliged to do so now and again, I've often wondered why I do it at all, especially as the longer I go on, the less my words appeal to my audience, for I am no critic, no keynote speaker. What's more, I harbour the suspicion that speakers are chosen for much the same reasons that you'd hang up a pair of new patterned curtains – you want to ring in the changes in some way, hear a different theme or tone for once. Now this is something that would make me uncomfortable even if I *liked* giving talks, because this kind of change doesn't interest me – I consider it fundamentally misguided. This might make you think that I'm conservative or, since there's not much left to conserve any more, restorative. But that would be a false assumption. So, since I have no enthusiasm for talking, and don't do it well, you'll have to excuse me if this doesn't quite come out in the polished form that you'd hear from a seasoned speaker, for speech is not my means of expression.

We'll have to see whether you'll find something that seems worth listening to, something you can take home with you, in what I have to say.

You have come here to discuss the professional concerns of your organisation. If I have understood correctly, yours is a cultural association, that is, the aims you pursue are more cultural than social. When I heard this, I was extremely pleased that a group of people in your line of business had banded together to pursue cultural aims. But then when I looked at the matter more closely, from various angles, I got the impression that you would (after all) be very reluctant to sacrifice your commercial prospects for the sake of your cultural aims. But I'd like to say that this sacrifice is one that you would have the capacity to bear, that is, your stake in the 'Economic Miracle' would not have to be continually sacrificed to culture.

Ladies and Gentlemen, the question is now, What *are* your cultural goals? Have these changed, are they in need of improvement, are they being achieved? Moreover, can you do business in this way, and how will you do business tomorrow? The cultural ambitions that you have are not just for your own internal consumption – a kind of private hobby – they also have an economic role, and imply a particular attitude towards society. In fact, I'd like to go further and say that cultural aims are the expression of a world-view. It is just not possible to say 'I would like everything to mesh in a beautiful, harmonious way', or 'I find that tasteless', without considering the background to these pronouncements or being clear about who they apply to. We've gone beyond the time when furniture-makers tended to split into two camps: one supplying the rich man with his representative luxury (in styles ranging from some Louis or other to Swedish birch burl with tubular feet), the other producing oversized, vaguely domestic revival style bedrooms, with bells and knobs on, to be bought on the never never after an encounter with a cunning smooth-talker, otherwise known as an 'experienced salesman'.

Your organisation evidently has other aims: *you're* not who I was just referring to. I've also noted with great pleasure that you don't sell the so-called whole '*trousseau*', but only individual pieces that can be combined according to need. At least that's the theory; whether or not it's your actual practice is something I can't judge. Whatever the case, it reflects an awareness that is worthwhile and correct. And this *alone* puts you in the real avant-garde of the furniture business.

It means, however, that those of us who are at the leading edge of design, myself included, are another kind of avant-gardist – a species which is not understood by the commercial side, a species which makes things that the consumer rejects, and so can't be put into production. That's just *one* of the reproaches levelled against us, the other one suggests exactly the opposite, namely, that we'd like to make things in such a way that their form and function are fixed once and for all and are therefore unalterable. Or at least more or less unalterable, in that any change arises from a slow process of fine-tuning. So there's no total transformation, as in the fairy-tale's frog-turned-prince, but a gradual evolution based on improved knowledge.

So what should one make of such ideas, and what do we as furniture designers expect of you, the people who distribute the furniture, the members of the Neue Gemeinschaft für Wohnkultur?

Since you are a cultural organisation we will begin by considering the cultural aspect of the problem and ask ourselves: *Why furniture? Why beautiful furniture? Why functional furniture? Why mass-produced furniture? Why reasonably priced furniture? Why furniture that corresponds to our times?* We'll find answers to each one of these questions!

Why furniture? – because our lifestyle requires us to have furniture to sit on, lie on, work on, store things in. Hence chairs and stools, beds, tables, cupboards and wardrobes. In an extreme case, however, you could imagine getting by with a minimal amount of this kind of furniture, since much of it could be built in, made a permanent, immoveable feature of the house, meaning that we'd have less to schlep around with us in our increasingly nomadic existence. There are some countries, such as the United States for example, where certain types of furniture like cupboards and bookshelves have practically disappeared from the market, because they are mostly built in. Given how widespread today's nomadic lifestyle is, furniture should be easy to transport and, in the case of larger pieces, dismantle.

The second question, *Why beautiful furniture?*, can be

answered very quickly by saying that beautiful furniture and ugly furniture cost exactly the same. To some extent, if you get the process right, beauty arises for free. At least that's how it must often seem, given that many furniture manufacturers have got into the bad habit of dispensing with the services of a first-rate designer, even though the designer places a relatively small burden on the production costs and, indeed, if the collaboration works properly, can even help to lower them. Since you are an organisation concerned with culture, you do not as a rule make the models yourself with the help of some cost-saving draftsmen and a few foreign interiors magazines. Making models that have no rationale and no character would run counter to your cultural aims, and would scarcely be tolerated by you. So you have beautiful furniture, with a cultural dimension, designed by first-rate designers, and you are an exception among manufacturers in being aware of the cultural importance of furniture. (I hope I'm not mistaken here.)

And now you're marketing these fine pieces of furniture at affordable prices, so that anyone whose taste has not been completely ruined buys their furniture from you almost as a matter of course, and is always happy to be advised by you. So we reach a kind of edenic state where everyone is happy – even your designers, who are given the licences for their work.

Now the next question, *Why functional furniture?* At first one might think that this is a question that answers itself, that furniture is functional in any case, that it's obvious one can sit on a chair or eat at a table. This all seems self-evident to us too. But we believe that functionality ought to be seen as something more than the *bare* fulfilling of the purpose – it's about meeting the requirements *completely*.

Of course you should be able to eat at a table. But you also need to be able to do other things with it too (though eating alone brings a whole host of things into play). You want the table not to wobble, not vibrate, to stand firm and yet not be too heavy; you want it to seat varying numbers of people, have a surface that can be used for all kinds of things but still always look good; you want to be able to make the table quite small, or conversely extend it, place it in a corner or have it freestanding in the middle of the room, and you want to be able to take it apart when you move. In a nutshell, the poor table has to be able to do everything, fulfil every purpose, and on top of that be beautiful too.

I have to confess that I've made a number of tables myself, and none of them manages to incorporate simultaneously every single one of these demands, though I really tried to achieve this as far as possible. What we're trying to do is find solutions that can be used universally, until the time when we're finally able to devise standard solutions that complement each other while fulfilling their own specific functions.

It is a similar thing with the chair, a piece of furniture that in recent years has been the subject of the most varied experimentation. For all this, the purpose of the chair is quite manifestly to be sat on. But this sitting is very varied – in both type and duration. The point is to single out, from all the variables, the ones that you want – and need – to respond to, if the chair is to fulfil its function. And this function gives a certain direction to the form, determining whether it's high or low, broad or small. Working within these constraints, you finally arrive at the form that is the most accommodating – for sitting, cleaning, transporting, manufacturing. Each of these requirements suggests a whole range of possibilities, and yet in the end only one of them will correspond completely to the task. It's hardly any wonder that so many kinds of chair are being produced, all of them quite different, all of them more or less fulfilling their function. I say 'more or less' because no one's producing chairs that you can barely sit on any more. And yet you still come across some borderline cases. These mostly arise when the designer gives free rein to his famous imagination and common sense falls by the wayside. In such cases, the designer misguidedly allows himself to give expression to his own fantasies instead of creating a chair that can withstand all reasonable criticism and in the process fulfil its functions completely – including its function of standing as a beautiful object in space, and looking equally beautiful whether it's in use or not. So that would be the answer to the question, *Why functional furniture?*

And now *Why mass-produced furniture?* It seems almost redundant to raise this question in this age of industrialisation, and yet it hasn't quite been resolved in relation to furniture manufacture. We're still haunted by the theories of handcrafted furniture, with so-called industrial products being seen as not entirely valid substitutes. On the other hand, industrial production is a fact of life, and in furniture-making especially it's practically impossible to maintain the distinction between the hand-crafted object and the industrial product, as both employ almost identical means. In fact, in some cases the same model of mass-produced furniture is not just made by a single firm but is produced by a number of smaller workshops, or in various countries. The boundaries are therefore blurred, as long as you are talking about models which could be produced using traditional carpentry methods.

But there are also new methods of production which can only be applied if huge sales are anticipated – where the initial costs of setting up production are so high that the same model has to serve as the basis for a whole subsequent series, even though it cannot be substantially altered once it's in production. I could mention a well-known cup chair that is being produced in the United States after considerable outlay: it isn't particularly practical (though it looks all the more elegant for it) but it cannot be improved – it simply has to be offloaded as it is. Moreover, the start up costs are so high that the chair cannot be sold at anything like a reasonable price, but is just as expensive as an individual piece crafted by hand. From this example you can see that in furniture manufacture both serial production and industrialisation are governed by their own peculiar laws which vary according to the individual circumstances and can never be schematically anticipated. The point of serial production, and the point of a standardised product, is to exploit an experience, or rather sum of experiences, for as long and as intensively as possible. This means that once you have a valid model you make it available at an affordable price to the largest number of people, thereby raising the general level of culture. This illuminates the need for greater care in preparing the initial model. With serial production, you can't be bringing new models that are more modern or fashionable onto the market every year; instead, you have to develop a basic model to a really high standard and then fine-tune it once it's in production.

This leads to the next question, *Why reasonably priced furniture?* Reasonably priced, as you know, means that the price reflects the input into the product, making it worth what you pay. But this doesn't mean cheap, just as it doesn't mean expensive; it means quite simply a decent price for a decent service. We know that furniture cannot be gratuitously cheap if we want it to be durable, for furniture is sold to last for a generation, after all. But on the other hand reasonably priced furniture is only reasonably priced in relation to its performance, that is, any superfluous element, anything that raises the price without increasing the performance, adds to its cost without making it more valuable. Lately people have once again been advocating adding ornament to 'create value'. I would like to expressly warn the Neue Gemeinschaft für Wohnkultur against this.

It is a mistake to believe that things either should or can be decorated with some kind of embellishment, even if this comes down to some simple profiles and ledges. These additions are and always will be unnecessary ballast; they create only confusion, and never added value. As an organisation you are of course more concerned with cultural values than with the material values that are implied in this type of ornament. But ultimately you have to make a living too, which brings you dangerously close to the territory where carpet manufacturers begin to produce value by the kilometre, the makers of furnishing textiles join in, and before you know it furniture-makers end up going the same way too. I'm speaking hypothetically, but it has already happened.

And unfortunately, even though you're a cultural organisation, your members have not remained wholly unscathed by 'value-creating ornament'. Perhaps one of the reasons why I accepted the invitation to talk to you, even though I'm not so keen on making speeches, is that I wanted to be able to tell you what was said by a whole generation before me, in ever new variations: namely, it is not *our* job, and not *yours*, to make standard everyday objects easier to sell by adding superfluous kitsch; rather it is our common task to make these objects in such a way that they *serve people in the best, most lasting and beautiful manner possible*. And it's precisely this so-called 'value-creating ornament' that diverts us from this fine task. Shouldn't we ask why? Because there's a reason behind all these things – they don't just arise out of thin air.

In my view this has come about because up to now we haven't been able to develop a truly valid standard for utility objects and above all furniture. Instead designers approach every commission as a kind of one-off, with the ulterior motive of making something striking to show off their great ideas. There's a kind of competition to be original. As a competition, this can be fine, and I wouldn't want to argue that nothing useful ever comes out of it. But unfortunately experience shows that it rarely does. I would prefer the competition to be turned around, with a call for people with really bright ideas to apply themselves to making a chair that is simple, practical and comfortable, for example, or a table that doesn't wobble. This requires a much higher level art than all the other stuff, all the neo-Baroque money-spinners and acclaimed 'free forms'. For whereas it's easy, if you have a little talent, to ride the tide of fashion, it's much harder to make something completely normal, sensible. Even those who are in a position to design something (ie who aren't just concerned with stirring up excitement for the latest models in the trade journals) find it hard to go back to basics when it's so much fun to make something overtly avant-garde – that's just the nature of the creative process. Everyone who works in this field finds themselves thinking at some point or other that they'd like to express what they 'feel', create their own style, leave their imprint on everything they make. I see this as one of the major obstacles that has to be overcome if we're ever to reach an acceptable standard. When they're working on something, designers should not be thinking about the opportunities for self-expression: the only measure they should be applying is whether the object does its job completely. For it's only in this way that the object will acquire a character that is particular to it – a character related not to the designer, but to the object itself.

It is up to the designer to decide how to reconcile the purely functional demands with the use of materials and the economic constraints. There's a personal element in this, related to their sense of artistic and cultural responsibility, but the idea of value for money also comes into play. For an object that is given a final polish by an artistically disciplined designer gains something that surpasses any artificial addition of 'value-creating' ornament. It gains an intellectual integrity.

What I've set out for you here is a new point of view. Though it is still relatively untried in practice, I'm convinced that it will form the basis for design work in the years to come. So, to sum it up once more, I should emphasise that the designer has to step back from the work so that the object's form expresses not his character but rather the character of the task. If we reconsider the idea of 'value-creating' ornament from this perspective, then we can see that it is nothing more than a prop that has been pulled out of the junk room to divert attention from an apparently hopeless situation. As Adolf Loos put it some time ago, ornament is planted wherever something isn't quite right. Things haven't got any better since. Whenever something doesn't work as it should, an attempt is made to cover it up with decoration as a way of making us forget that it doesn't perform its task. However, we like to engage with these tasks and we endeavour to solve them. If I say *we* here, I'm speaking for the friends and colleagues at Ulm with whom I set up the Hochschule für Gestaltung in response to both a need and a sense of duty in relation to twentieth-century culture.

Our approach to solving these tasks is not to simplify the problems, as the arts and crafts movement did; it's not the traditional way, but rather the approach that I've just presented to you. We are deliberately trying to be as restrained as possible in our creative work, in order not to repeat the mistakes that have shown us just how *not* to do it. Clearly we cannot take some existing style as our starting point but must instead investigate the functions anew, for it's only in this way that we'll find the direction for our research. In principle, however, if our findings turn out to be confirmed in the form of a Biedermeier chair, there's nothing to stop us from simply developing this chair further (without feeling the need to launch into the world a totally new construct in some *recherché* kidney shape).

And in connection with this I'd like to move on to the last question, *Why furniture that corresponds to our times?* This question seems to me almost harder to answer than all the preceding ones. For how should we define our era? What measure do we use to say what is in keeping with our times? Ultimately we cannot use machines, cars or aeroplanes as such a specific measure. One speaker at a recent conference on 'industrial aesthetics' defended the streamlined style on the grounds that it was a new kind of decoration that captured our contemporary lifestyle, which is bound up with speed and flying. Fine, but it's entirely superficial and wrong-headed for manufacturers to then apply this so-called streamlined style to prams and flower vases.

Other critics of our times chip into the debate with the complaint that everything today is far too technical, so the home has to become a kind of refuge – something best achieved by modelling its interiors on those of our great-grandparents.

Comparing these two extreme positions, we can perhaps say that each one in itself has the semblance of being correct: you could even go so far as to say that both are correct to roughly the same degree: so you have streamlined trams on the street, and Biedermeier side-boards at home. I believe that such confusion is *understand-*

able given the difficulty of the situation we find ourselves in. After all, man has evolved over the course of a few thousand years from living in caves to consuming nuclear power. This is not such a long time-span in which to make such an enormous leap. So it is hardly any wonder that you have whole tribes, whole segments of societies, that have reached different levels of civilisation and have different needs. All of them consequently have a different relation to what we call 'our times', depending on their specific situation. How does this situation relate, then, to our question, *Why furniture that corresponds to our times?* For me this question is redundant. We don't know what kind of furniture corresponds to our times, for we don't want to make furniture for our times – we want to make furniture for people. We don't want a culture for *our times*, but a culture for the *people who live in these times*. We live in the present – that's a fact – and from here the only way to move is forward. But we are not concerned with this, we are concerned with doing our job.

So, within the short time available, these are roughly the answers that I can provide to the questions that interest you, as members of the Neue Gemeinschaft für Wohnkultur, as much as they do designers. These are primarily cultural questions. But cultural questions have wider ramifications.

I have heard some people say that designers, with their extreme views, have no commercial sense at all, and that if things were left to them the furniture business would never survive. But then how come it's so hard to go into a furniture store and find things that are simple, good, practical? People end up buying things they're not entirely happy with, or that are too expensive. Or how come people are always complaining about being ripped off? I don't know whether you experience these things too. I hope not. But I can't quite rid myself of the suspicion that even you sometimes dally with things that are not quite in *bad* taste, but aren't in the *best* taste either, so long as it's good for business. Otherwise, how would you find things in your catalogues that cannot unreservedly lay claim to cultural worth? This is the seed of a conflict that we could easily argue about for days. But I believe that wouldn't get us very far, for perhaps you really do see the things that I'm alluding to as commercial necessities. To prove the opposite would require setting up a trial where our two different conceptions competed under the same conditions.

To this end, I wouldn't want to suggest that you should abandon *all* of the things that you have learned to value up to now. What I think is that, in addition, you should attempt to stock another kind of furniture and objects and promote them in your usual way, working to assemble a collection of things that could be character-ised as standard – as opposed to modernistic gadgets (which you may rightly want nothing to do with, or may even misguidedly like). I'm thinking here of things that are honest and good, that serve their purpose in the best possible way; things that are at the same time perfectly beautiful – but not in the fashion of the moment; that perhaps change only slowly, through continual fine-tuning. If you do this, I believe you will be able to fulfil your real role and aims as a cultural organisation even better than you're already doing today – that is, you'll be helping broad swathes of the population to live more enjoyably, comfort-ably, harmoniously. I know that this programme will encounter some heavy opposition. Perhaps not from you, and certainly not from the consumers, but from the designers of the pieces you require. For there is not yet a widespread readiness to dispense with 'self-expression' – to create things that are anonymous and have character precisely because of this. This is a problem of education, and it will never be resolved so long as every technical school still clings to the belief that every single one of its students is a genius destined to bestow upon the world some kind of totally new form – rather than insisting that their most talented students should apply their skills with discipline and common sense. That's what we're trying to do at the Hochschule für Gestaltung, and we are willing and ready to work together with you, the Neue Gemeinschaft für Wohnkultur, in the way that I've just sketched out, in order to get closer to the goal that stands before us – cultivating a way of life for our times.

WHAT IS INDUSTRIAL DESIGN? (1954)

The theme of this conference can be viewed in different ways. Having worked for years in this field, both theoretically and practically, I've taken a stand on the various issues up for discussion. And having spoken at a few conferences like this one, I feel rather like a parrot, endlessly repeating myself. My arguments don't change much, nor, it seems, does the composition of my audience: most of you will have already heard me speak several times about the problems I'm now going to address.

Last year at the conference on industrial aesthetics in Paris I concluded my talk with four propositions, which I believe could provide the basis for moving our work forward today:

> 1. The task of the artist is not to express himself and his feelings in a subjective way; it is to create harmonious objects that will serve people.

> 2. Artists, as part of their responsibility for human culture, have to grapple with the problems of mass production.

> 3. The basis of all production should be the unity of functions, including the aesthetic functions of an object.

> 4. The aim of all production should be to satisfy people's needs and aspirations.

What does all this mean?

With the first proposition I'm saying that the artist should take a stance *vis-à-vis* contemporary problems.

I'm talking about the artist. Perhaps this is a bit vague. You could be asking: What is an artist? What is art? What does 'taking a stance *vis-à-vis* society' mean? It's hard to come up with a good definition of these expressions, but I want to try anyway.

With the second proposition I'm asking that artists, 'as part of their responsibility for human culture, should grapple with the problems of mass production'. Here I'm assigning artists a role they've perhaps not had before. At the same time I recognise that mass-produced objects can be, and ought to be, of a cultural order, and that artists are responsible for achieving this.

With the third proposition I'm setting out a direction for production. I'm saying that it has to 'achieve the unity of functions, including the aesthetic functions of an object'. This means that producers have to be in agreement with the specialists in culture: with artists.

The fourth and last proposition is the most important one, the basis and end-goal of all these efforts: 'the aim of all production should be to satisfy people's needs and aspirations'.

This last proposition is also the key to today's theme of 'industrial design and society'. It means that each object should serve people, and just as people make up human society as a whole, so these objects should fulfil a function in our societal life.

I believe we can generally agree on the substance of this fourth proposition. But what is much less clear is the definition of 'people's needs and aspirations'. We know only too well that these are as diverse as people themselves. Nonetheless, our analyses indicate that a large number of needs can be categorised as common needs. That is to say that everyone has the need for a bed, a plate to eat off, a roof over their head – objects that represent a minimum standard of living. But there are also categories of people whose needs are greater, and in the overall framework of things their needs are valid too.

As for people's aspirations, diverse as they may be, they still display a common yearning for well-being, security and peace (inner and external), a desire for a standard of living that makes life joyous and free, both economically and physically. This shows that our thinking cannot be isolated from social issues. The things that we're concerned with are in effect cultural or artistic problems.

We maintain that the whole endeavour of design should be directed towards serving people. This is an important statement, since there is a competing conception of what design is all about. This concept deploys the notions of 'industrial design' or *esthétique industrielle* or *industrielle formgebung*. If we take people as the focus for all efforts in *design*, these notions are all false, but if we take as our goal the prosperity of industry and commerce, they are quite valid. As for everyone here, I suppose we're all in agreement that industry should not be an end in itself, but should serve humanity. What we hope will result from the processes of production are objects that serve us as well as possible and at a reasonable cost. The means of production depend on various technical and economic factors, and it essentially makes no difference whether an object is made by hand or by machine. It's the function that counts, although this function may be divided into several sub-functions.

One of these sub-functions is the cultural function of the object, its form, its *good form*. This is something more than the simple aggregation of the different functions. Evidently we're not concerned here with things that have no function to fulfil, completely useless things, knick-knacks in a modern or old-fashioned mould. We're interested in useful objects that are at the same time objects of perfect beauty. This is what is declared in the third thesis: 'the basis of all production should be the unity of functions, including the aesthetic functions of an object'. 'All production': ie, by hand or by machine. 'The unity of functions' means not the aggregation but the integration of all functions, including the aesthetic functions, thus the integration of cultural functions with daily needs.

Now's the moment to consider the meaning of the second proposition: 'artists, as part of their responsibility for human culture, have to grapple with the problems of mass production'.

Artists have a 'responsibility for human culture'. What does this mean? Quite simply: artists, as experts in culture, are ultimately responsible for culture. One could object that artists don't have the power to fulfil this function. Or one could say that artists are isolated in ivory towers and shouldn't expand their remit beyond spiritual questions. It is possible that many people truly believe that it is the role of the artist to be a hermit, a living anachronism, producing so many square metres of canvas covered with colours and motifs that have no meaning beyond individual self-expression. It is no exaggeration to say that 95 per cent of painted surfaces and sculpted volumes have frankly no other purpose than self-deception – or the blatant deception of the public. You may think this is going a bit too far. But I ask you to think of the average exhibition – you'll find very little there that would qualify as 'art', putting aside any considerations of style, modern or otherwise. It is not these artists – these compulsive, mediocre tricksters – who should be occupying themselves with culture in general. Rather, it is the true artists who need to take responsibility for culture. My statement concludes: 'they should grapple with the problems of mass production'. This gives the true artist a true function in society. I don't want to detract from art as the highest expression of man's spirituality, but I am taking aim at the belief that art is somehow detached from everyday problems. I will return to this issue later when I speak about education.

But now I'll quote the first proposition again: 'the task of the artist is not to express himself, but to create harmonious objects that will serve people'. This is a condensation of what I've said up to now. If I speak against 'self-expression', it's because what we want from an artist is a form of expression that is not purely personal but instead has a certain objectivity and a reason for being. And when I speak of 'harmonious objects that serve people', I'm not excluding paintings or sculptures from this – although these works of art belong to the category of objects that have a single, well-defined function, pushed to the limit: effectively, they could be classified as objects with a spiritual function.

So those are my propositions and supplementary observations. They may seem rather theoretical. To make the subject more tangible, we need to study a concrete case. As an example I've chosen, not a specific object, but an exhibition – the Milan Triennale. All of us who have an interest in this exhibition, now in its tenth iteration, are asking: What is its purpose? What function does it fulfil? What's the best way to move forward?

I'd like to begin by relating some of my own experiences. I've curated the Swiss section twice, in 1936 and 1951. It is always enjoyable to take part in an exhibition like this and to pit your ideas against those of your colleagues from other countries, as in a sporting event. Yet on both occasions I found it extremely difficult to find objects to put on display. It seemed the most viable form of participation was simply to be present with our business card – more or less paying homage to our dear Italian neighbours. Not much of a starting point, but that's how it was.

The reality was also that our participation was of very little interest, economically speaking. The outlay on the installation far exceeded the total cost of the objects on display. There was an imbalance between investment and result. Perhaps it was the choice of objects that provoked this negative outcome. However, I believe that other countries experienced the same problem. And in truth, it was not this economic factor that really bothered me, but more the absence of utility – the fact that there is absolutely no need for an exhibition showcasing decorative and industrial modern art and modern architecture.

You may have noticed that, in my vocabulary, decorative art has negative connotations: I always empha-sise *function* and *culture* in its place. Perhaps this is my default position as a purist: I hate this so-called decorative art. Yet it is precisely this decorative art that has always filled the Triennale and that is once again consuming hundreds of square metres of the present show. It's not only filling the display cases, not only lurking behind some of the most grotesquely shaped furniture – and a ridiculous modernism – it's also climbing the walls and covering the floors and ceilings too. With all the murals, tapestries and reliefs – figurative, abstract and concrete – there is no space left for relaxation, for calm. In the absence of harmonious objects with artistic merit, piles of fussy objects vie for space with pretentious garbage.

Frankly speaking, I would have trouble selecting five per cent of the objects on display as positive examples for a special exhibition on a social theme – whereas I could find any quantity of things to serve as bad examples. I recognise that people's viewpoints vary, but personally I can see no reason for displaying these decorative knick-knacks, which serve no purpose in today's society and culture.

Of course some of the participants in the Triennale, for example the Nordic countries and Holland, demonstrate a particular concern for the needs of man. There's also the exhibition of industrial design, which seems to me to serve a purpose, even if a number of the objects on display are embellished with modernistic lines or pointlessly encased in aerodynamic shells – they're not art, nor are they aeroplanes.

Finally, looking at the garden, we see some nice ideas that are well presented. Two of the formats seem particularly successful – the pavilion on water, displaying naval constructions, and the sgraffito labyrinth. Thinking of why these two pavilions are the ones that impressed me most – along with the displays of industrial design, musical instruments and the Spanish pavilion – I'd have to say it's because each represents, in its own way, a well-defined programme and attempts to strike a perfect balance between a specific theme and the overall exhibition programme and objects on display.

But one could question whether it is really the task of each Triennale to come up with a few good concepts for exhibiting work, or whether this is not quite its purpose, and not in itself sufficient to justify such a huge outlay and effort. I won't disguise the fact that I no longer believe in this kind of exhibition. But when you ask me what should take its place, I have no real answer. The solution is hard to find. There are all kinds of difficulties: how do you unite the participating countries, artisans and decorators under a single central theme? And how do you approach this theme every three years? But this is not solely an issue for the Triennale, it's more or less a problem with exhibitions in general. What's lacking is a special theme that relates to society as a whole. If you want greater success, then you need to have greater coordination among the participants and better defined, more exact themes. I believe that all countries could adopt the approach used for the exhibition of industrial design. As things stand now, with a jumble of trends on display, you get the impression that you've stumbled into a department store selling decorative art.

The other solution would be to hold a straightforward fair for functional objects, devoid of decorative art and focused solely on *good form* with various sections devoted to furniture, lighting, tableware, etc. I'm sorry I have no magic solution to offer for the future of the Triennale. All I'm saying is that decorative art can no longer fulfil the functions it used to, or that we once thought it did. It's a mystery what we should do with all these useless things, produced only to waste money – a superfluous cult. There's certainly no point in putting them on display and suggesting to the public that they have a material or even a spiritual value, responding to our needs and aspirations. I believe we should try to redefine the role of the Triennale in relation to society. How could it fulfil a very important function, both informing and educating?

In the first part of this attempt to fuel a debate I outlined some propositions. In the second part I criticised the look of the current Triennale. Finally, in the third part, I'm going to say a few words about education.

Immediately after the war I criticised exhibitions that lacked an educational purpose and at the same time I proposed a form of exhibition that would be a synthesis of information, instruction, excellence and enjoyment, a form of exhibition that wouldn't wear you out but interest you.

I know this is an extremely difficult agenda to realise. But we have to do so if we want to get out of our current impasse, which threatens to stymie the whole purpose of exhibitions.

If I singled out the labyrinth in the Triennale garden, it's because it represents a kind of synthesis of critical reflection, humour and special effects, created without recourse to mediocre decoration. In addition, the Triennale's section on industrial design manages to be instructive as well as effective and easy to understand, communicating its particular concept with the simplest of means. These two very different examples demonstrate the various directions you can go with research, aiming either at *instruction* and *education*, or at the creation of an ambiance that reflects the chosen theme. In the end, it all comes down to the theme and the objects that are going to illustrate it. And here we come back to the starting point of my talk, where I spoke about the role of artists and their responsibility for culture both now and in the future.

It's a question of education. For a long time I have stressed that true artists need to concern themselves with the problems of mass production. There's already a certain contemporary tradition of great artists influencing the production of functional objects. It's what happened at the Bauhaus, where personalities such as Kandinsky, Klee, Moholy-Nagy, Albers and Schlemmer taught. They had an enormous influence, as their doctrine was disseminated through their students.

Since then no other school has matched the influence of the Bauhaus. As a conseqence, the importance of its approach – experimental, drawing on the field of art in the creation of functional objects – has been overlooked.

But now we've begun to recreate this kind of instrument of coordination with an institution that is a continuation of the old Bauhaus, but takes account of today's conditions and needs – that translates the idea of the Bauhaus into the present day. This is the Hochschule für Gestaltung in Ulm, which is now in the process of moving into its new buildings. A pilot group has been there for nearly two years, with a group of students of different nationalities working in the fields of architecture, urbanism, information, visual presentation and product design, which covers the creation of all functional objects. We hope that this new school will be able to make progress and that we can foster this type of artist-creator who will be, and can be, responsible for culture both today and in the future.

DEFINITION OF THE
TERM 'PRODUCT FORM' (1957)

I coined the term 'product form' in 1950 to describe products whose characteristic feature is their form.

A product is everything that is made by man, irrespective at first of its form. A product in this sense can be a city, a house, a machine, an appliance, a book or a text, but also foodstuff. It is the form that gives you an indication of the kind of product that you're dealing with. The form is the semantic expression of a product, ie, form in this sense has, *a priori*, an informative character.

What I understand by form, particularly in relation to product form, is explained in the following text, 'Function and *Gestalt*'. Similarly, what I say there applies also to the concept of form in relation to the product, that is product form.

The combination of product and form is however more than the simple conjoining of the two terms, which only partly explains the new term of product form. Rather, product form has an autonomous existence and in future will be applied primarily to use-objects in the widest possible sense.

FUNCTION AND *GESTALT* (1958)

There are doubtless any number of issues that seem much
more pressing than the one I'm going to talk to you about
today. For example, there's the pollution of the waterways,
or traffic planning, or the problem of land use – preserving
open spaces on the one hand versus increasing densifica-
tion on the other – there's also automation and its impact
on social structures and culture.

All these issues are of course extremely urgent. Our
material well-being depends to a large extent on resolving
them in an appropriate way. And there is a causal connection
between this material well-being and the personal freedom
of every individual. But still we have to ask: what are we
doing with this material well-being both today and in the
future? Is maintaining it the sole purpose of our existence?
Is the mechanistic, now almost rote preoccupation with
preserving our lifestyle – which is often just a sham – sus-
tainable in the long run anyway? Is this any kind of natural
state? Or, indeed, how do we define a 'natural state' today,
in an age of technology, or tomorrow, in an age of supertechnologies? In other words, not yesterday, on some South Sea
island, but today and tomorrow, here in Europe.

Of course this is something we've all applied some
thought to. Everyone has already tried in their own way
to solve these problems for themselves. For many, one or
other of the established religious schemata – the belief in
an unknown X – can offer respite and in some cases also
aesthetic sustenance. But what once stood as an aesthetic
bound up with the practice of religion – as the ideal of
aesthetic perfection – has become a thing of the past and
cannot be recovered through modernisation or reinterpre-
tation. Times have moved on, and people's expectations
and habits have changed.

Since we can only move forwards from the present, and not back, there's little point in pondering how or when, or by which external or internal causes, people became 'decentred' – or perhaps didn't after all, depending on what you mean by 'centre'.

Even so, it's quite obvious that our well-being does not depend purely on our material existence, though this is indisputably the driving force behind most people's lives. However, it is equally indisputable that our material existence only acquires meaning if the life of the mind is given the same kind of weight. This intellectual dimension is readily apparent in the pure sciences and the arts and is most evident, perhaps, in the so-called fine arts and generally in what we like to call *visual culture*. The thing that we call art is only one component of this visual culture, yet it has a considerable impact on our environment. The environment, in turn, has a decisive impact on people's well-being, from which we can conclude that art occupies a key position within our mental and spiritual world, in the sense formulated by Hegel in his aesthetics, namely that art is the form of human expression that speaks of the highest interests of the Spirit.

Hegel's definition might still hold – and perhaps even be more valid than ever. For at the time Hegel was writing, the full possibilities offered by art were not yet apparent. And, reading his writings on aesthetics, it also seems certain that, if he were around today, he would not allow himself to be appropriated as the star witness for so-called socialist realism.

Now, I have maintained that the environment, and the art within it, is of great importance for the human spirit. You will say we've always known that. And yet it seems necessary to emphasise this fact today, given the brouhaha that is gathering around technology. It is being said, quite rightly, that there is a shortage of engineers and technicians to help plan for progress. Great prospects are being held out for the technical professions. There is talk of new educational routes, of all the problems that will be solved by training more technicians. And there is some shock (not wholly unjustified) at the huge technological advances being made by the superpowers of America and Russia.

But here I have to repeat the question: what is the point of this massive expenditure on technology? I'm hardly a luddite, I simply want to provoke some reflection. What is really going on? Has spending all this money not become something of an end in itself, perhaps (yes, certainly!) making us forget the flip side of the coin? Our environment doesn't just need to be equipped technically, it needs to be *designed*.

The problem is that environmental design is not vital to the export industry. It produces neither nuclear reactors nor calculators, both of which are very important to people. Environmental design is merely intended to create an environment in which people feel well, physically and mentally. There is certainly a purpose behind this. And this purpose is something we should not forget.

In recent years a recognition of the importance of the environment has led to an investigation of more exact ways of approaching its design. Above all, an attempt has been made to define new methods where the designer's personal taste and abilities (or lack of them) would not play as great a role as it has in the past, with more built-in safeguards, as in technology.

In order to get a clearer view of these problems, it is necessary to address questions of aesthetics, function, *gestalt*. Before I move on to the real significance of tonight's theme of function and *gestalt*, I'd like to explain to you what I understand by function, and what in my view is meant by the term *gestalt*.

Although these terms are common, their meaning varies depending on the field in which they are used. There is a conception that the term function, strictly speaking, refers solely to a mathematical function. This has come about because Leibniz, the founder of the mathematical concept of function, discovered, in around 1684, the algebraic functions of differential and integral calculus; that is, the variables whose value depends on the value of another variable. Leibniz's term was then broadened further in mathematics, to the point where the discipline is now inconceivable without it.

Correspondingly, then, the term function denotes the behaviour of one incidence in relation to another. It describes a correlation. In mathematics this correlation can be expressed in numbers, and for this reason mathematics and logistics represent the ideal field for the purest theory of function.

In its broader, more general sense, however, function means the relation of one thing to another. Therefore, when we speak about fulfilling a function, we are talking about producing something to fulfil a need, or simply fulfilling a function using appropriate means.

Getting to the bottom of the term function, we can see that it in no way has a restrictive sense, but incorporates among other things the mathematical function. The term function is therefore an umbrella term for the relations of things to each other.

This forms the basis for my understanding of the term function, which I've set out briefly as a way of approaching its implications in relation to the term *gestalt*. This conception of function goes beyond that of causation, though I also view causality – the relation of cause and effect – as a part of function. Causation is the basic premise of the theory of function. The relation of cause–effect is in turn the outcome of function. I will come back to this later, when I attempt to define *gestalt*.

By function I therefore understand a relation, for example the relation between material and form (whereby a material's physical properties do not initially need to be taken into account). Functions therefore consist of several relations. They can stand for a number of demands, since in practice 'function' is generally translated into the 'demands made of something'. For example 'the function of an artist in society' or 'the function of a chair' (in relation to the person using it). Or 'the function of traffic planning (*vis à vis* an urban structure). Function always refers to the relation between a minimum of two variables that are dependent on each other.

The mathematical concept of function, as defined by Leibniz, Riemann and Weierstrass, forms the framework for an extended conception of function. This concept is the abstract schema that practice refers back to and that also forms part of the general linguistic use – into which could be ranged, ideally in an orderly correspondence, all uses from 'to function' to 'functionary'.

But that is not the sole purpose of this extrapolation. More pressingly, there is a need to find an objective viewpoint from which to assess certain categories that are otherwise difficult to bring together, particularly within the framework of aesthetics. That viewpoint is the relation of people to things. In this context the focus of interest is not so much the world of things given by nature. Rather, it is the world of man-made things that has to be investigated in order to explain certain phenomena, such as the existence and meaning of artworks. Or the existence of motorised vehicles. Or the existence of electronic calculators. And so on. And not only as isolated phenomena but primarily in terms of their interrelations.

In this connection we can distinguish two different groups of functions.

The first one reveals the relations between the object and people as individuals (and as a society).

The second one reveals the relations between the components that make up the object and the processes by which it is produced.

To illustrate this point I would like to use a perfectly simple object: an armchair. Its relation to people consists in the fact that it is designed to be sat on. The manner of sitting can vary. Visually this is expressed in its form. But whether or not a chair is good to sit in – comfortably, or for a long time, or whether or not one can relax – none of this is immediately obvious from its appearance. Yet all of these are factors that we designate as functions – as relations between a person and a chair.

Yet even when it's not being used, the armchair still has a visual presence. As such, the relation between man and chair is also an aesthetic one. It has an effect on the human psyche. Thus its form is also a function, and when it is consciously designed, this aesthetic function has a great impact.

A further relation consists in the price of the chair, its affordability; that is, in whether it fulfils its economic function, which is for it to be purchased. And then there is a final generalising, social function: the chair must be usable by different kinds of people: small ones, tall ones, fat and thin. It must – to refer back to the aesthetic function – also work when produced in large quantities, and not just as a one-off piece. Ultimately its designed form must be able to fulfil its aesthetic function not just in relation to other pieces like it but also in relation to the people who use it and the various other objects in our environment.

That is one side of the story: the relation between people and chairs (which can also be described as the satisfying of a multiplicity of demands).

The second group of functions, covering the relation between the components – material, use, means of production and so forth – is directly dependent on the first group. If we again consider the example of the chair, this means the relations between the possible materials of production – for the frame, the seat, its texture, the texture of the surfaces, etc. And these again relate to the cost of manufacture, which in turn has an effect on the production run. Processes of production–material–price–sales all stand in a causal relation.

In the same way, there are many possible means of production for many possible materials, which again affects the performance of the real function, ie the relation between man and object. The more exact the definition of these functions, the clearer the requirements, then the more unified the result will be. The requirement for this unity or harmony now becomes a cultural requirement, in so far as it is also an aesthetic problem. The result is visibly manifest as form; its unity as *gestalt*.

Here, by form, I mean that which we can see in space. If we conceive of the term form in this very particular way, then, when we hear the word, we associate it with something that displays characteristic features corresponding to typical functions. More precisely, we sense from the outset that the word form designates a certain quality. We take it to be almost self-evident that form equates with beauty.

In this sense we perceive all the positive appellations – 'the perfect form', 'the beautiful form', 'the good form', 'the useful form' – to be positive variations of one and the same quality, namely the formal quality; whereas descriptions such as 'the ugly form' or 'the useless form' contain an inherent opposition that immediately expresses something negative, namely the lack of formal quality. We criticise form in accordance with the principle of beauty – deliberate, accentuated beauty.

When we speak of natural forms, we have in mind forms that are especially perfect and in accordance with their kind – typical. Such typical forms we name *gestalt*.

When we speak of forms of technology, we have in mind forms that we specifically deem to be valid, elaborated solutions, rather than just any old technical outcome.

When we critically assess the form of everyday utilitarian objects, our constant yardstick is whether or not the form works as the 'harmonious expression of the sum of all functions'. This means neither an artificial simplification nor a streamlined style that runs counter to function. It is, rather, the natural, self-evident appearance that we specifically perceive as form and hence as beautiful. Forms arising in this way, as the harmonious expression of the sum of all functions, disclose the outward characteristics of their type in their *gestalt*.

With an artwork, the fact that we understand the designation form in direct relation to specific stylistic characteristics means that form is an irreplaceable component of the artwork, and that an artwork counts as an artwork precisely by virtue of its form. Thus form, in its autonomous existence, represents an idea which becomes *gestalt*, and through this becomes identical with art. This also explains why form is always evaluated in relation to something else – as being more beautiful or less perfect than another form – and why ultimately perfect beauty is a measure for form just as it is for art. So, here too, form ultimately strives to be an expression of beauty. Since form implies the sum of all functions in harmonious unity, and form is like art and like beauty, one may readily conclude that art can also be defined as the sum of all functions in harmonious unity, and the same applies to beauty.

Now these things may seem perfectly ordinary to you. I too am of the opinion that they ought to be taken as self-evident. But unfortunately this is far from the case. It is not easy to find objects in our environment that have been designed according to these principles.

Experience shows that it is not quite as simple as people think to develop an everyday object so that the final form is the direct outcome of all the demands made upon it. There are three constant dangers lurking on the path of development: 1. decorative arts; 2. so-called popular taste; 3. functionalism.

By *decorative art* I mean something which is applied to the object with the express intention of creating something beautiful – and which more or less gets in the way of its real functions.

By *'popular taste'* – in inverted commas! – I mean not what consumers generally want, but rather what manufacturers think is easiest to sell to them.

Finally, *functionalism* (like any other -ism) is prone to dissembling. It acts as if its aim is to fulfil all functions. In this respect it can be seen either as an offshoot of decorative art, saddled with the same deficiencies, or as a pseudo-solution reduced to the purely material functions.

These well-worn paths will never lead us to *gestalt*. What we'll arrive at instead, time and time again, are houses, vehicles, implements that are subjugated to short-lived fashion trends and riddled with unresolved problems. These products do not have a valid *gestalt*, not in the way that I understand *gestalt*.

Here I've used the term *gestalt* in a quite specific way and set it in relation to function. I repeat: *gestalt* is the sum of all functions in harmonious unity. In other words, *gestalt* is produced from the coordination and integration of all functions, as with the example of the making of a chair that I referred to earlier. This process consists not only in researching possible outcomes, but also in making a selection from them.

The first step is made easier by the application of *morphological methods* of the kind Fritz Zwicky has investigated for technology as well as other fields. The second stage is a process of selection in which the most disparate functions (not least the aesthetic one) are applied as criteria.

At present we're just feeling our way in this. Max Bense, professor of epistemology and philosophy at the Technische Hochschule at Stuttgart, has outlined some promising methods that seem to offer a sounder basis for aesthetic judgements than empirical observations.

But we can't yet know whether these efforts will ultimately lead to anything. People have long dreamed of treating artistic phenomena on a scientific basis. But it seems to be precisely a characteristic of art to always remain one step ahead of this scientification.

Now one could object that all these constraint-inducing considerations have little to do with creative activity. And perhaps you're surprised to hear such digressions from me, a defender of artistic freedom. However in my experience such freedom is not so much limited by natural laws as secured by them. Incorporating the aesthetic function into the overall functional development of an object leaves relatively little scope for *free decisions*. But one can be more certain about making these decisions when the functionally determined possible solutions are clearly laid out.

Opponents of such an approach point to the role of intuition and the striving for freedom in design. They would have us believe that only works arising out of the emotions are fully valid. Others, by contrast, are trapped in the belief that the sole guarantor of validity is a so-called scientific process. They believe that the form of an object will automatically arise from the aggregation of the most essential functional demands.

I am convinced both conceptions are wrong: what is required is not only intuition (which plays a necessary part, moreover, in a work of pure engineering) but also a process of synthesis based on careful analysis. What is required, therefore, is a third way of achieving a result that we can then call *gestalt*: besides the specialist knowledge that can be written down and learned, one needs training in aesthetics. What is required is a knowledge and a recognition of aesthetic methods of selection and, on top of this, the instilling of an aesthetic sensibility, which cannot be learned from books or replaced by calculations. The basis and the measure for aesthetic evaluations, however, lies partly in the workings of the so-called liberal arts.

As a way of picturing what I'm saying, I ask you to think of a diagram that starts off by encompassing the sphere of the intellect: that is, thinking, feeling, imagination, in short, the world of what is thought and imagined. At this stage, all things are still immaterial and not transferable – they are merely present as energy.

Communicating what is thought and imagined requires additional energies besides language: these can be directly perceptible as sound or light, or they can take the form of impulses that relay information with the help of instruments.

So from this intellectual energy centre we move in two opposite directions that loop around to form a circle and overlap. The looping of the circle encompasses the made world, our *environment*. On the one hand we have technology, starting today with electronics, on the other hand aesthetics, starting with the most immaterial elements, music and language. Both electronics and music require instruments of a technical nature; they become perceptible (although obviously not physically manifest) through the use of instruments.

In this way energy, here already partially materialised, begins to take part in the process of making. At the same time an interplay begins between the aesthetics of technology and the technology of aesthetics. And once again it is the function between technology and aesthetics that is decisive. Picture the diagram with technical components dominating one side and aesthetic intentions the other. Running down the axis between them are use objects and architecture. Whereas almost everything in the realm of technology can be achieved with the aid of calculation plus intuition, in aesthetics a careful training is required to build up an operating base. Moreover this training presupposes a considerable honing of thought processes, and the training itself is closely tied to what I'd like to call a systematising common sense. How to undertake this training is a pedagogical problem which has to be considered in terms of its impact and desirability, as well as in relation to other pedagogical problems.

If we think back to the circle that schematises the man-made environment, then we see technology on the one side and art on the other. Step by step they lead towards each other, and one could perhaps envisage the ideal picture as one where the breadth of the circle remains constant, ie any reduction in technology is balanced by an increase in art, and vice-versa. Hence what I'd like to call the 'functional density' remains constant. And, further, both ends issue into the sphere of the intellect, the immaterial, which we can equate with the energy that fuels creative activity.

I ask you to keep this diagram in mind when we consider the problem of education and training. If we accept that art has a spiritual function – which is, in Hegel's terms, to realise the highest interests of the Spirit – then technology has a material function, which is to provide the best possible basis for our material well-being. If we draw a line between the two poles of technology and art, it will touch not only on the highest interests of the human Spirit but also, equally, on the facilitating of material existence. And it is along this line that our everyday use-objects lie.

As some very useful research has demonstrated, we now find ourselves in a situation where education in the technology sector is lagging far behind our needs. This is not a new finding – for some years now there have been warnings about the consequences of disregarding the primary role of training in the field of technology, and especially in creative technology. With the new supertechnologies, just operating a run-of-the-mill kind of calculator requires a higher set of skills than our technical schools could provide 20 years ago. The growth of technology calls for an extraordinary increase in technical aptitude – just to maintain existing levels of comfort, never mind take them further. What I mean here by taking them further is finding ways to make complicated things more simple, in the context of processes becoming inexorably more complex.

The issue of nurturing technical talent is undoubtedly of exceptional importance for our development. It would be too much here to enumerate all the expected consequences of technical stagnation (which incidentally are gradually entering the general consciousness). But the most immediately obvious consequence would be that the national economy, starting with certain sectors, would lose its competitive edge, leading to a gradual decline in living standards.

All kinds of plans are now being drawn up for the reform of technical education. The most interesting boil down to this:

> 1. there ought to be a general reform of the educational system, including high schools and colleges;

> 2. from this a cadre of technical personnel could be developed;

> 3. this should then form the basis for a more universal education.

Thus we have come to realise that in the long run it is not enough to train only good and averagely gifted technicians. There has to be in addition a top tier, an elite. However this can only emerge if the overall standard of technical education is relatively high and provides the conditions for the imagination and knowledge to develop in complete freedom. Here free means disengaged not from practice, but from the necessity to come up with instant results. This kind of attitude towards technology can be found in many instances, to be sure, and needs no further commentary. Also crucial is a joy in experimentation and, finally, not only a good academic record but also the kind of character that does not shrink from difficult tasks.

Although I am speaking to you about function and *gestalt* in relation to artistic problems, I have to refer back to the complementary arena – technology – to illustrate the conceptions and tendencies that prevail there and show how these could be nurtured in the educational sector.

In the area of art the situation is quite different, as it is in the intermediate fields.

There is ample provision for environmental infra-structure, since it is clearly vital for the national economy. The damaging effects of a malfunctioning environment are also addressed with gusto by the medical and pharmaco-logical sciences. On the issue of whether the remaining natural sciences could be as effective in preventing the damage in the first place, the jury is still out. One possible clear exception is physiology, which is increasingly having a say in the material improvement of workplaces and equipment. Thus the equipping of the environment more or less proceeds apace.

Much more problematic, however, is the situation of *environmental design*. In this field the training structures are so deficient that they are quite incapable of taking on greater responsibilities.

But whereas the problem of education is already giving serious cause for thought in the field of technology, in art it has barely penetrated the consciousness of those in charge. Very few are aware of just how serious it is. And this problem is closely related to the long-winded explanation of terms that I tried to entertain you with earlier, in an effort to clarify the fact that what we under-stand by the term art has changed – has had to change – and that art fulfils a new function whose effects are different from before.

Without doubt the field of science and technology has been in a state of upheaval for around 50 years now. Paralleling this, and bringing it into the intellectual consciousness, there has been a break in the tradition of philosophy – brought about in a large part by Nietzsche, Husserl, Nikolai Hartmann, Bertrand Russell, Whitehead and Wittgenstein. Epistemology as a branch of philosophy has provided explanations for the new development. From this, new knowledge has emerged, and along with it a new critical attitude towards technical phenomena.

A further parallel development can be observed in the field of art and, beyond this, in environmental design. Yet it seems to be taken much less seriously, as if it were a kind of private matter for the initiated. There are people who view architects as some kind of nebulous entitities – necessary to help build buildings but prone, in the process, to trying to smuggle in ideas whose value is not always appreciated. And admittedly this mistrust is not always unearned. All the same, it's kind of alienating to find some venerated captain of industry using the occasion of a lecture on nuclear energy to launch an impromptu all-out attack on modern art, pillorying its practitioners as charlatans – partly because of their attempts to explain art in relation to similar developments in the material sciences.

For art can no longer be regarded in isolation. And if I call for art to be integrated into daily life, what I mean by this is not that much-vaunted recent marriage of painting, sculpture and architecture. Nor do I mean public so-called support for art. Rather I'm thinking of the application of the knowledge that is derived out of free experimentation in the so-called liberal arts. This knowledge can inform the design of our environment from the level of the spoon to the city.

The new art is a reality and its impact since its creation has been greater than is generally assumed. If episodes like the one I've just described still occur, it's because there's not yet a widespread recognition that structuring the environment doesn't just come down to providing for material comfort; it's also about connecting people with a designed environment that allows for the life of the mind, in keeping with the much-trumpeted notion of progress.

There is a recognition that the cultural impact of the environment has to be taken seriously – and by environment I mean from the smallest object up to the city and beyond, even to the region, as well as the individual contemporary artwork. This recognition was long ago raised to the level of a demand, but up to now insufficient means have been applied to carry it through.

And yet culture is not just the private concern of the individual, but a matter for democratic society as a whole. And such a culture cannot be fetched ready-made out of a box room; it has to be created, worked for and lived.

What's so unsatisfactory about the situation today is the widespread lack of the kind of insight that is required to implement a progressive cultural programme. Instead there is a belief that art and the things related to it, from architecture and planning to the industrial product, are more or less a matter of individual initiative – even when it comes to education.

This also explains why, if someone has taste, a little aptitude for drawing and painting, and manages passable academic grades, this aptitude for painting and drawing then becomes the proof of a creative spark, signalling a destiny in architectural studies, as a future creator of culture.

Of the trajectory of the painter and sculptor, who in the Renaissance still belonged to the ranks of the learned, it's best not to speak here, since it's a particularly depressing chapter. But in connection with today's theme I do want to mention those anachronistic souls who haplessly seek their education at a school of industrial arts or so-called vocational academy (*Werkkunstschule* or *Werkakademie*).

Experience has shown that only a small portion of those educated in this way can make a meaningful contribution to the overall development of culture, but in the current transitional period they still form a possible

basis to fall back on in time of need. But what about those
people who are rightly dissatisfied with what has been on
offer up to now, and who want to assume the duties and
responsibilities of creative work, in the sense outlined
above? Where can they turn? Or what about those who
have had to schlep around the ballast of a pseudo-art from
the outset of their careers, but now realise that a knowledge
and experience of the methods of design must also embrace
the notion of social responsibility?

Ten years ago I set up the IPC (Institute for Progressive Culture) to undertake experiments and coordinate the
findings with the quite general aim of promoting a culture
appropriate to our times. The path that we took led to
exhibitions highlighting the issues involved, to publications
and to pedagogical experiments of various kinds, including
the founding of a new school whose curriculum was
conceived to respond to the needs of contemporary culture.

All these experiments pointed to certain findings
which can be summarised as follows:

1. There is a need today for an institute that specifically addresses the problems of aesthetics as they
apply to practical life (an idea reflected in the original
working title – Institute for Practical Aesthetics).

2. Such an institute needs a solid economic and
intellectual base (the economic basis has to be
provided by the state, the intellectual basis by able
colleagues).

3. Such an institute is viable only if it is directly linked
to other institutes of higher education, otherwise
there is a risk it will attempt (amateurishly) to tackle
problems that could be better addressed by technicians – in the process neglecting its true tasks, namely
those of aesthetics and design, and failing to fulfil its
purpose. Such tendencies already posed a danger at
the Bauhaus: many of the painters there would tackle
prefabrication, for example, without having the

necessary technical grounding. And in recent times similar tendencies are again becoming pronounced.

4. Such an institute must bring together all those subject areas that are grounded in the development of an aesthetic practice – and in all areas their shared methods must be developed in common, as a matter of basic research.

5. A decisive role in the development of this foundation is played by practical tasks, which help to clarify lines of thought and are essential to the creation of a workable theory.

We know that such an institute for practical aesthetics is needed now more than ever, and it is to be hoped that one of the existing schools will decide to take a step in this direction.

The requirements outlined here are not new, but are in a sense a further development of an educational system that in its time was the basis for an educational institution – the Bauhaus – which had a pioneering influence far beyond the boundaries of Germany. Brought to life in Weimar in 1919, when Walter Gropius transformed an existing art school, it had to move first to Dessau and then finally to Berlin where, as a private institution, it was closed down by the authorities in 1933.

But it's a little dangerous to evoke the Bauhaus of that time, since only a few people today know exactly what went on – and it stands before everyone else as a myth. Myths, even relatively recent ones, are impediments to development, as they cloud one's view of reality.

But it would be unjust if I were to fail to point out that, in principle, there is no difference between what the Bauhaus was trying to do then and what I am trying to do now. What *has* changed is our level of knowledge and the conditions in which we operate.

The nearest we currently have to this programme are the curricula of departments of architecture in the technical universities. But we all know that these are sorely in need of reform. Perhaps a more apt comparison would be with an institution such as a college that is affiliated with an institute for occupational physiology or management science.

Experience has shown that the whole field of design in the sense of today's theme of function and *gestalt* is too wide-ranging to be easily encompassed within a regular course of study. For those who are particularly gifted in design, ie for an elite, the starting point for their education must be to acquire knowledge and experience of existing theories and practices. This in itself makes such an education incompatible with the contemporary curriculum of a college of higher education, and more likely to fit in the framework of an institute.

I am aware that a great deal of water will have to flow under the bridge before a programme like this can be implemented, even in a diluted form. But in this age of mass production the alternative – inaction – could cause incalculable damage. We're already getting a clear sense of this today, as we discover that it takes longer to recover from a cultural decline than a technical standstill.

The required financial investment would be much lower than that associated with contemporary technological projects. The 'sum of all functions in harmonious unity' arises to a certain extent for free. What it calls for, above all, is exact thinking and correct behaviour and – crucially – extremely able participants. Because it requires a continuity of personnel, this way of operating is much harder and more expensive to achieve than one-off pieces of technical equipment. And this is probably the reason why no such institute exists up to now.

To address some possible misunderstandings, I must again emphasise that our desired goal – an environmental design that fits with contemporary needs – cannot be achieved by decorating our environment in a superficial way, with modernistic gimmicks in a streamlined style, an earlier tendency that is now being revived and channelled towards Europe mainly via American designers. The

difference between what is being sought there and what
I am calling for is encapsulated in the contrasting titles of
two publications: the American star designer Raymond
Loewy's *Never Leave Well Enough Alone* [original English
title: *Ugly Doesn't Sell*] and the Swiss brochure *The Good
Form*. And this oppositional quality is found not just in the
titles, but also in the contents.

Precisely because we need to exclude this easy-to-
follow route, our aim is harder to achieve. But this should
not deter anyone from striving for an ideal condition in
which all the man-made things in our environment, from
the smallest utilitarian object up to the city, are in the same
way the 'sum of all functions in harmonious unity', ie are
gestalt, and thus a self-evident part of daily life.

Such a condition can then unhesitatingly be described
as the culture of our time. And that's what we're striving
towards.

MANAGING OUR ENVIRONMENT (1960)

The imperatives driving our management of the environ–ment ought to be well known by now, since they've been a focus of concern for almost 50 years. We have never ceased to evoke them forcefully, sometimes appealing to reason, sometimes to ethics.

Today these principles need to be recalled, and more clearly than ever. But before we can discuss them, we have first to articulate them. Once they've been articulated, we'll have a basis for debate. We'll have a thesis whose meaning we can then elaborate. In instances where it is apparent that in principle nothing has changed, we'll look at the reasons for this failure, and seek ways to remedy it.

Modern man is beginning to find it natural to have at his disposal effective means of transport. He is no longer astonished to have water, gas and electricity in his home. He lives in a comfortable world. He believes he's leading a secure existence. To him, everything seems to be for the best. There would be no point, then, in asking him whether everyone really has a fulfilling part to play in social production, or whether his sense of security has a common quantifiable character, given that everyone seems more or less happy with their lot.

For all this, we believe many things could be done differently. Man finds it easy to adapt. He is always looking to adapt every new situation to his needs. His spirit of invention has brought us to our current levels of achieve-ment in culture – in technology, art and science. His efforts have created an artificial world that is subject to perpetual change. According to the laws of cause and effect, new possibilities give rise to new conditions in society – as well as new complications, which man always and continually seeks to overcome.

Thus our culture grows, like a web of need/order/ disorder, spiralling into chaos. And man is so adaptable that he ends up feeling quite at home in this chaos, and even attempts to organise it. We've gone so far down this road that chaos is now seen as a particular form of order. There is an element of truth in this, to the extent that chaos can be organised by compiling lists, noting and classifying its different elements.

But this chaos has grown so much in recent years, become so lavish in its dimensions, that we now find ourselves trying to accommodate it – only attempting small interventions when it seems we have no other choice.

And I'm not just thinking of traffic chaos. The chaos of production has also reared its ugly head. And I'd rather not speak here about the chaos of construction in our towns and countryside, the chaos of the property business, the chaos of water management, the chaos of noise.

Despite his great organisational abilities as an individual, man has not yet managed to master these diverse forms of chaos, that is to say, he has not yet found a form for society that would allow each person to be free without prejudicing the natural interests of his fellow man, indeed, without generating chaos itself. This is not simply a legal and political problem, but a moral and aesthetic one.

Finding a solution depends on the development of a general consciousness – which still seems a long way off, given that our rational thought processes are not governed by a single integral concept but are instead rooted in isolated, scattered ideas.

These preliminary considerations are necessary in order to demonstrate that these particular problems can neither be treated nor resolved in isolation. They spring from a much larger concept which does not begin or end with the management of our environment on the one hand, or its configuration on the other.

What we affirm is this: man may well be adapting to a continually changing environment, but the fact remains that, physically, human beings do not change that much. While noting changes in lifestyle, we can observe that the simplest actions (walking, sitting, sleeping, etc) remain unaltered. The basic physiological conditions are still the same: it's just their form that imperceptibly submits to the changing conditions of the environment.

Whether man is working, resting, busy or, as that felicitous expression would have it, 'idling', his well-being depends on the functioning of the objects around him – on objects of daily use, tools, machines. This dependence is not only physical. Objects also have psychological associations. They can be defined either separately or in relation to their surroundings, to other objects, or to those who use them.

Regarding the requirements – physical and psychological – of these objects, these can be split into two groups.

1. Those requirements which are related to the objects themselves, and which correspond fairly closely to the demands of 'the good form' (*die gute form*) – the benchmark accorded annually by the Swiss Werkbund in collaboration with the Swiss Fair at Basel.

2. Those requirements which concern the manufacturers, ie industry; the middlemen, ie commerce; publicity, ie the press.

I shall develop the first point according to the guidelines I've set out for defining 'good form'. These are the qualities that we should demand of well-made objects.

1. The object
By object I mean something made by man, either by hand or in a factory, a one-off piece or a mass-produced item. These are objects in daily use, such as furniture, all kinds of utensils, machines, appliances, tools, sports equipment, construction elements, means of communication, etc.

2. Utility
The object, as far as possible, should fulfil all the functions for which it has been created.

3. Usefulness
The choice of material and means of production
should serve to enhance the usefulness of the object.

4. Suitability of form
The external form of an object and each of its
constitutive elements should accord perfectly with
its intended purpose.

5. Aesthetic unity
The form of an object should not simply be calculated
in response to its use, but should be manifest as a
harmonious whole, evoking a general impression of
beauty.

6. Cultural good = useful form
The aesthetic function, being the visible expression
of all the functions, is the decisive argument for
classifying objects as cultural goods for our time and,
consequently, as 'good form'.

Moving on now to the second group of requirements:

The mere fact that we have guidelines allowing us
to judge whether objects are well made does not in itself
mean that we've made much progress. The 'good form' that
we discern in this way is often less distinct in a mediocre
object than in something with an appealing appearance.
However it is quite distinct from a useless object.

While we note that the initiative of 'good form' has
yielded a series of positive results, it would be an exaggeration to say we are satisfied. We do not merely want to have
useful objects that are not too ugly. We want them to be
perfectly useful, as well as especially beautiful.

Unfortunately we are still a long way off from this
goal. But it's not entirely our fault. Part of the responsibility
lies with the manufacturers, who are content merely to aim
for a relative improvement. And what should we say of the
retailers and their continual attempts to put a brake on
development? It's time, too, that we denounced the passiv-

ity of consumers, the fact that they're not informed – for which the press must be blamed.

Nevertheless we have to acknowledge that in recent years the press has waged a few bold campaigns with very satisfactory results.

These experiences have allowed us to define the second group of imperatives:

a) Well-made objects should grow in number. They should be promoted officially both here and abroad.

b) Swiss industry should strive – especially in view of the 1964 national expo – to produce objects that demonstrate a level of progress, that don't just go halfway towards meeting the requirements for 'good form', but fulfil them entirely.

c) Industry has to be open to specialist advice, so that Swiss products can be recognised not simply for their high technical standard, but also for the quality of their form.

d) The 1964 national expo has to judiciously adopt these guidelines for the definition of good form. If we're articulating these ambitions today, it's because we are convinced that the future does not belong to chaos and its beneficiaries. We believe that the world in which we live could be less spoiled, better and more beautiful than it currently is.

Unfortunately industrialisation has transformed our environment for the worse; more than that, it has destroyed the nature around us. It has a detrimental impact on the normal course of human development, yet at the same time offers certain advantages that should be made available to everyone as we enter an age when we need to repair, by means of a global culture in which art has its place, the damage wrought on nature.

WHAT IS GOOD ABOUT
THE GOOD FORM (1961)

An endless stream of self-regarding claptrap has recently taken the place of reflection on things and what they mean. Dissimulation, hair-splitting and intellectual posturing are the order of the day. Even design jury members admit they evaluate the things in front of them according to their own preconceptions rather than any objective standards. And in this disorder, figments such as 'the good industrial form' flourish.

It's worth taking a closer look at this term. What does 'industrial form' actually mean? Is it something good or bad, nasty or ugly, or beautiful? In fact, 'industrial form' says nothing. Something has form, or it doesn't exist. It doesn't have 'industrial form'. Unless that's supposed to mean the form of the industry, its production methods, its organisation or even its products?

The term 'form' is a different matter. Form is intrinsic to every object, every material, everything that we can perceive. To anyone who doubts this, I don't feel that I need to explain here for the hundredth time what form is. I summed it up in a few words in my book *form*,[1] and Eugen Gomringer expanded on this a short while ago.[2]

The term form was originally combined with the word 'good' in order to emphasise the utilitarian nature of form, to highlight the self-evident form (and not with the intention of creating a slogan). This 'good' stands in opposition to ugly, useless, bad, nasty, and has the implied characteristics of useful, practical, functional, usable and even beautiful.

The fact that 'the good form' (*die gute form*) became a slogan is not the fault of the endeavour behind the term. If some people have misunderstood its meaning, it's their fault alone. If some equate 'good form' with a kind of fashion trend, it surely has to be put down to stupidity. And then there's the mania for deploying the various permutations of emphasis to express different moods or desires – or pedantry or mischief: '*the* good form', 'the *good* form', 'the good *form*'. Everyone who experiments with this emphatic nonsense concludes that none of the three emphases can be intended or allowed; only their equivalence makes sense. Their conception that 'the good form' has never had anything to do with 'design-lite' is made quite clear in Margit Staber's essay, which quotes fully my own 'evaluation guidelines'.[3]

But it has to be admitted that even the best guidelines can guarantee nothing. It all depends on how they're applied by the members of the jury. And in my defence I have to say that I've had no influence over those jury decisions for years now, and many of the objects that have won awards wouldn't have got my vote under any circumstances.

Although 'the good form' was never intended as an absolute mark of distinction, in the beginning we still hoped that the overall standard of commended objects would continually rise and that the guidelines could be more strictly applied. In reality, however, the procedures employed by the jury have been in need of revision for years.

When it comes to assessing how good 'the good form' is, it is necessary to distinguish between two things: 1. its meaning and aim, 2. the actual practice. The meaning and aim are outlined in the 'guidelines'. The practice lies in the hands and heads of the jury members, in their experience and conscience. It may be a bit depressing if the 'good' part of the equation sometimes seems barely to scrape into that category, or is no longer in evidence at all, but this is not a reason to condemn the endeavour as a whole.

This is not the place to judge the ceaseless hum of activity emanating from design congresses, design schools, design managers or design juries. Ultimately they're all just swarming around the honey-pot of industry, and unfortunately their output is often self-conscious and contrived rather than guided by natural processes. Design exhibitions and reviews are being pulled along by this same current – a regrettable development, but not a tragic one, because in spite of this (indeed often because of this) things turn up now and again that merit the appellation of 'good form'. And 'good form' doesn't have to mean boring, contrary to what the prophets of doom from the neo-rococo circles maintain, their gaze set firmly on the 'value-creating ornament'. Sometimes, though, these criticisms seem to be not so far off the mark, and they're given ample reinforcement by the 'square-cross-section' fanaticists and pseudo-rationalists who together have demonstrated that the 'modern' doesn't need to be remotely connected to the good form. All those who strive to make good things can derive some consolation from this.

But whether 'the good form' is good or not depends wholly on the quality and decency of the designer and the producer. I don't want to invoke the well-known dictum about doing the decent thing. What is decent is perhaps well and fine, but it's not sufficient to make a form good. Decency is one of the starting points for good form, the bare minimum, which is just about tolerable because it's not indecent. But making the good form good is purely a question of design, a question of the ability to coordinate and order – the ability of the designer and those who are responsible for production. In addition it requires a capacity to use one's aesthetic knowledge to find a way of counterbalancing all the irregularities that arise both naturally and technically, and bringing them together in a harmonious whole that is typical of its kind. In this moment making something good is a question of decency, to be sure, but at the same time it's one of ability too.

1. Max Bill, *form* (eine bilanz der formentwickung um die mitte des XX. Jarhunderts), Werner, Basel, 1952.
2. Eugen Gomringer, 'die gute form', lecture published in *typografische monatsblätter*, Berne June/July 1961.
3. Margit Staber, 'die gute form', in *form* 14, 1961, p. 45 ff.

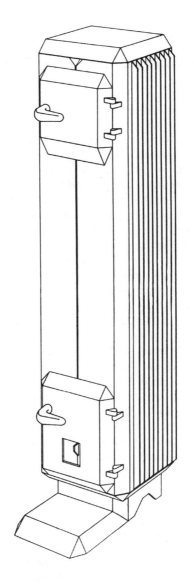

Design for a radiator, 1963

MAY A HEATER BE … A HEATER? (1963)

The question seems pointless, a no-brainer. Why shouldn't it be? Or why should it now, after all? In the days when a briquette oven was an oven with no pretensions to be a piece of furniture, any attempt to make a heater into anything other than a heater would have been viewed with terrible suspicion. The ornamentation of the time may not always have been meaningful, but a heater was … a heater.

But today the briquette oven is – we freely admit – no longer the pinnacle of technical achievement. Nowadays there are all kinds of ostensibly more advanced sources of heat. Elegant objects have been produced, more elegant than any oven up to now. Nonetheless the charcoal oven remains by far the most widespread single heating device in Germany, and the individual heater is by far the most widely used heat source of all.

For some time these heating devices have had trouble adapting to 'the tastes of modern times'. Initial attempts at blending the heater into Mr Average's interior resembled outsize pancake griddle pans made of brown enamelled cast iron, with a twee gilded grill. Just the thing to go with the Gelsenkirchen baroque living room suite and matching dressing table and gramophone set. It's different today. Today such a heater is supposed to be compatible with the latest products from Grundig, if not quite the output of Braun. It can even be produced in an alleged Bauhaus style, or an even more alleged Ulm design. It may be modern, with the 'designer' appropriating its form from the refrigerator (which often needlessly produces heat – cold through warmth) or the dishwasher (yet another heat-generator). In this way it is brought into line with 'modernity'. And not just through its external styling, heaven forbid, but also through its function. Convector oven, forced air circulation, heated air-flow: the air rises up over it and is warm. Oh wonder of wonders! Not only that, the air rises between it and the liner, which encloses its actual form. This moderates the temperature on the outside. The advantage is that you can no longer burn your fingers on the casing – one less life-experience to chalk up. But with the thing as a whole you can certainly get your fingers burnt – at least figuratively. Thus the air streams from the floor to the ceiling – where it becomes nice and toasty. Since most fireplaces are not located in a wall with a window (the optimum location for central heating radiators) but internally, this circulation of heat takes place at the back of a room, between floor and ceiling. The circulation of dust is also amply provided for. This is certainly a great step forward, especially when the instrument used to achieve it resembles an ice-box or a spin dryer.

The heater is now disqualified from its previous role – namely, to radiate cosy heat into a room – because it's compelled to look like something other than a heater. It's supposed to look like a warm cabinet … a heater can no longer be a heater. It's supposed to be a cultural act, an exhibition piece, even more than that: a promotional monument to the charcoal briquette. It's supposed to have a 'good industrial form', even when it no longer quite fulfils its intended purpose. (Or is the intention to use more briquettes to produce less heat? Surely that can't be the plan?)

At the briquette manufacturers' association, or among the worthy members of the jury assembled for a competition, is there really anyone who imagines that the problem of the charcoal briquette oven has not already been addressed, indeed solved in a perfectly satisfactory way (at least technically) at least once, if not twice or more – as for example 50 years ago, with the pot-bellied stove? Does anyone really believe that a heater has to be something other than a well-conceived tool that takes up the minimum amount of space? As unassuming as possible, as small as technology allows, correct, uncluttered? A tool with an anachronistic-seeming function, but no modernistic anachronisms?

Should a modest, good heater really … should all other things in our environment also … should they? Count me out.

ON EXPENSIVE JUNK (1963)

Exactly ten years ago, at the first conference on industrial aesthetics in Paris, I gave a talk on aesthetics in the machine age. It was essentially devoted to problems of education. We'd just launched, that same year, the first foundation course at the school at Ulm, a course that I was to lead for a further two and a half years until my young collaborators – former students – would judge my ideas to be old-fashioned and unviable. In the meantime these same young collaborators have proved that their system is no more efficient than mine, to say the least.

This brief introduction would not be necessary if we had a clear and precise definition of the problem that I call *gestaltung* and that others describe as 'industrial design' or 'industrial aesthetics'. In fact I've become aware in recent years of a stark difference between what I understand by my term and what others understand by theirs. At that conference in 1953, I'd made fun of the notion of industrial aesthetics, which suggests that the point of aesthetics is to adorn industry. The same goes for design, and especially 'industrial design', which is thought to be at the service of industry. For me this is where the difficulty lies. It is right that creative work should adapt to the demands of today's economy, using the means currently available to industry, but it is wrong, in my opinion, that it should do so to profit the latter. As I keep on saying, our efforts should serve people, consumers, it's them that we should have in mind in creating an object of any kind. If this is the designer's function in society, then he has a responsibility not only towards his client, that is to say industry (the producer), but also, and above all, towards man (the consumer). It's worth recalling this from time to time, for it's understandable, even quite natural, that when money talks, morality hangs her head. And this applies most of all in 'industrial design', a domain that rubs shoulders with advertising, as Vance Packard's studies – *The Hidden Persuaders*, *The Waste Makers*, *The Pyramid Climbers* – brilliantly demonstrate. I can highly recommend these books, which construct a social critique of a supposedly free economy but are as easy to read as a detective novel or a threepenny opera.

But you are no doubt asking yourself what is the connection between these general considerations and the theme of the education of the designer, or rather the *gestalter*. I will respond that they are the key, the starting point of the problem. I define the *gestalter* in the following manner, as a person:

> capable of grasping and clearly presenting the problems of our man-made environment;
>
> capable of analysing them according to well-defined methods;
>
> capable of drawing conclusions from these analyses;
>
> capable of creating objects that respond to the function assigned to them by society or man;
>
> capable of constructing them in a way that maximises their usefulness and efficiency;
>
> capable of ensuring that their production corresponds with the available technical means, and is as economical as possible;
>
> capable, finally, of uniting all these factors in a harmonious whole which clearly expresses this unity, that is to say, the *gestalt* particular to this object.

This definition probably differs from the one that 'designers' and aestheticians would come up with. I also tend to be accused of being ideological and unrealistic. People believe that I claim to have invented, with my system, the only possible shape for a teacup or a fork, an absolute shape to last for all eternity. That has never been my intention; I'm only trying to resolve any problem in the best, most enduring way. I think it's completely gratuitous to invent a new model each year, a new styling, with the sole gratification of making the 'waste makers' even richer. I feel a responsibility towards society and every individual who is part of it, and as a consequence I refuse to exploit them by proffering shoddy, short-lived everyday objects – expensive junk. Unfortunately, that's exactly what industry tends to deliver by the truckload – at least that's what I think.

Certain people may find it excessive to place this notion of responsibility (towards man, towards society) at the forefront of the *gestalter's* education. All education, one could say, has at its root a feeling of responsibility, but for the *gestalter* it's an essential condition. We may concede that the place of the designer in our society is at the crossroads of the professions of advertising, architecture and engineering, but the real *gestalter* is situated next to the last two, and his work has nothing remotely to do with advertising. Therefore, bearing in mind his responsibilities, I believe that it's necessary to develop his human qualities as much as his professional capacities. That is why I have always insisted on the need for a broad education with a distinctly humanist stamp, which will give the *gestalter* the means to consider the particular problems that occupy him from the larger perspective of a man who is conscious of his duty towards society – like a pilot steering towards a better future.

There are doubtless many ways of inculcating a sense of responsibility. However, one of the most effective seems to me to consist of regular discussions, completely open and very detailed, about the results of the work; the need to always have to justify the direction you've chosen is an excellent way to develop a sense of responsibility. In my opinion these discussions are as important as the work itself, provided they are directed by tutors capable of giving them the necessary depth. In this respect, the education of the *gestalter* is a question of the personality of the teacher. A method of education based on personalities doubtless has its weakness, but it is the only viable principle in a field where the character of the individual plays such a defining role.

This is the human aspect of the formation of the *gestalter*. There is another aspect, which relates purely to his professional training. On this matter my experience has led me to repeat again and again that the apprenticeship of the *gestalter* has to begin with a trade. This may seem redundant in the age of the machine and automation, but it's hardly a taste for romanticism that makes me insist on this. It is simply that students who come from a practical background have proved themselves superior to those with only a theoretical training. Another equally important point relates to intellectual formation. In effect, the *gestalter* needs to have a solid knowledge of all kinds of fields if he wants to be able to tackle and resolve all the problems he will face. We now have more or less a consensus on the kind of knowledge that is required, and it's on the syllabus of those rare colleges that can be counted as progressive. Finally, professional education should be related as much as possible to reality. The ideal, to my mind, is to work on real problems in close collaboration with manufacturers, for any theory in this field can only be a product of practice, and all we can hope to do is to establish a doctrine of education, a working method for creating objects for daily use.

Saying this, I'm beginning to sound a bit like a parrot. Yet the more I say it, the less I'm followed. However, give or take a few small modifications here or there, I cannot see the need – or the possibility – to change any of my views. Besides, these are not just my views. They have always been around in some form or other. All I've done is rethink them in response to the needs of our time.

Kitchen clock with timer, Junghans, 1956–57

Wall-clock: matt chrome bezel, white metal face,
chrome hands, Junghans, 1959

WHAT I KNOW ABOUT CLOCKS (1963)

I have a weakness for clocks, which must come from the fact that one of my grandfathers was a watchmaker and we had beautiful old clocks at home, carefully regulated by my father so that they always kept perfect time. As a child I particularly loved two of these timepieces: a wall-clock and a pocket watch.

The wall-clock was in a modest empire style. I especially liked it because its face, with its figures and hands, was unusually graceful, while its pendulum and weights were particularly simple. This wall-clock had something about it of those precision time-keeping instruments that you find in factory gatehouses. Only it was more finely crafted.

The pocket watch had a special feature that never failed to delight me. When my father pressed its top, it chimed the hour and the quarter-hours lightly and softly, with a gently purring precision. The face and hands of this watch were also especially beautiful in terms of their configuration and fabrication.

Any clocks or watches that I've since come across have always been set against these two 'ur-clocks' from my childhood, and only rarely have I found one that could compare. Even in the *locus classicus* of the clock, Switzerland, it has been difficult to find anything new that has satisfied me nearly as much. In exhibitions I've been asked to curate, for example, at the Milan Triennale, I got into the greatest difficulties with pocket- and wristwatches: I liked the cases of some of them, the faces (minus the numerals) or the hands of others, but were all these elements related to each other in a harmonious way? Rarely, perhaps never. (Only the very expensive watches made by Vacheron & Constantin, or Audemars-Piguet, came up to my aesthetic standard, and it's only in the last ten years that an acceptable cheaper watch has come onto the market, the still consummate Juvenia.) All of them, however, had what seemed to me an essential flaw: their faces had no numerals. I could never be happy about that.

To say nothing of wall-clocks. The ones at Swiss railway stations were, and still are, the best. There's no messing around with them; it's all about legibility.

It was only through a kind of a misunderstanding, an accident, that I came to design clocks. I was still at Ulm at the time, helping to build up the School of Design, but on the way to getting myself booted out of the place. One day a man turned up and said he'd come on behalf of a watch manufacturer to ask whether I'd consider designing watches for his company: fashion watches. He'd seen an article with pictures of some sculptures I'd made and thought they could perhaps be the basis for a few sensational pieces of jewellery – a kind of endless ribbon with a built-in mechanism and the whole shebang.

I was less than enthusiastic about the proposal. But since I already had a drawing of my 'ideal watch' in a drawer somewhere, I explained to my amiable visitor that it would give me the greatest pleasure to produce some watch designs for him. Except they wouldn't be quite what he had in mind: no fashion watches, no seasonal throwaway trinkets. On the contrary, these would be as far removed from fashion as possible, as timeless as they could be without forgetting the time.

A brief was then established. The first item on it called for a 'kitchen clock with timer'. I set my students the problem. There were a few fixed parameters – it was to be ceramic, the mechanism was already there, the timer too – but something new had to be created out of them. One criterion, however, was non-negotiable: the thing had to have numerals – hours on the clock face and minutes on the timer. Why? Because the kitchen clock is often the only wall-clock in the house. Children learn to tell the time from it, learn their first numbers, the order of hour and day. And it had also to be as bright and cheerful as kitchen crockery. I made it light blue with a white dial and a white metal bezel. The firm asked for some other colour combinations. I considered a white one with a gold bezel just about tolerable, but in the end the light blue version prevailed. This outcome was initially not so certain. When we'd finished the prototype I'd taken it to the manufacturer in the Black Forest and the chief executive looked at the thing not with reluctance but (it seemed to me) no great enthusiasm. He took it away with him to show to the mayor of the town. The mayor eventually signalled his approval and some members of the board liked it too, so we were able to go ahead. Since then thousands of these clocks have been sold. And now, after six years of production, it's having a mini-makeover to iron out some small imperfections.

After this came other models satisfying further requirements by the company as well as my own desire to make clocks with numerals on them. Out of this came a wall-clock and matching wristwatch. I am pleased with the electric wall-clock because it is one of the clearest of its kind, with the big hand precisely marking the divisions of the minutes and the small hand indicating the hours. But the wristwatch corresponds even more perfectly to my ideas, with its steel casing, its silver dial, its differentiated scale with minute marks that at the same time count the seconds, and its full crown of figures at the top of its face. And what particularly pleases me about this wristwatch are the fine luminous hands and the luminous points that mark the quarters, with a double point at the top, at the full hour. Little things? Perhaps. But I believe that so much in life depends on these little things, and much also depends on the time that is measured by the clock. And that is why – along with the very able technicians and workmen of the Junghans factory in the Black Forest – I'm so obsessed with making beautiful, precise timepieces.

ARE EUROPEAN METHODS OF ENVIRONMENTAL DESIGN UNIVERSALLY APPLICABLE (IN ART, ARCHITECTURE, URBAN PLANNING, PRODUCT DESIGN)? (1964)

By environmental design I mean shaping the human environment with a view to creating decent living conditions. In this respect environmental design is closely tied to people's intellectual and emotional needs.

Environmental design is the polar opposite of technicalisation, which aims at securing and improving living standards from a material standpoint. However the two realms meet in our everyday surroundings. The function of an object will determine whether it belongs more to the aesthetic or the technical realm.

Objects that belong to the aesthetic realm range from the pure artwork (an object for contemplative use), through the most varied forms of housing, to the city and the region.

Objects that belong to the technical realm range from the computer, through the most varied forms of prostheses – machines – to the technical framework for manufacturing the objects that we need on a daily basis.

So we can say that environmental design encompasses our object-world and is shaped by a striving for harmony as well as a remarkable (specifically human) desire for beauty. Also included in this is everything that people do either to secure or maintain their own beauty.

For years now there have been attempts to develop design methods with a claim to universal validity. These methods are defined, first and foremost, by the ambition of giving the maximum number of industrial products a general market appeal. This trend, designed to facilitate the widest possible distribution of large production runs by large industries, is an American phenomenon. It does not aim for a design based on a better understanding of the function of the specific object. Rather, its focus is on the external packaging, as an auxiliary to sales and advertising. It is not to be equated with environmental design, but with propaganda – rather than satisfying needs, it stimulates consumption.

The older strand of product design, which has a richer tradition, originates in Europe. It is based on the principle of social responsibility and has a moral character, in so far as its practitioners have to assume responsibility for an important factor influencing people's health, namely their surroundings – health in the sense of mental well-being, arising from harmonious environmental relations.

But we might now ask how applicable this European experience is to countries outside Europe, and to what extent is knowledge gathered in Europe transferable?

The first thing to note is that environmental design still only accounts for a minority of our output, and the theory supporting it is neither fully formed nor universally accepted. We are therefore dealing with a working hypothesis, the basis of an attempt to keep the design of the environment moving along the right track. Our experience appears to validate this hypothesis. I myself operate according to its principles.

This working hypothesis proposes that each design problem can – and ought to – be analysed and resolved on the basis of its functions.

But these functions – as the relations between object and person – differ according to location and external circumstances. So different results will arise.

This variation arising from a logical and organic process is absolutely consistent with the development of European design, but in clear opposition to American-oriented methods of influencing the market. The difference is that in one case the aim is to satisfy demands in the most reasonable way, so as to help people. In the other case, demands are to some extent artificially stimulated, so as to increase industrial capacity.

For us, as Europeans, the question now arises: to what extent is manipulating and increasing needs, particularly among populations outside Europe, in the interests of those people?

We must also consider our own situation regarding environmental design: here chaos reigns, tempered only by a barely heeded theory and a narrow segment of practice. We're facing a whole range of challenges – from the social function of the artwork, through housing construction, to urban planning – that will require our utmost efforts to overcome.

It therefore seems to make little sense to want to export such conditions. This cannot be our task. But this does not mean that we don't have a task; it's just that this cannot consist in teaching others what to do. Instead, we have to develop and disseminate the methods that will enable each, in their own way, to achieve the optimum outcome. It is the quite elementary design principles that are worth disseminating – those principles that allow the right methods to be developed in response to specific needs and distinctive cultures, of which they serve as an extension, and not some totally alien imposition.

How we can achieve this is not something I want to go into today. It comes down to an educational problem of the first order which, if left unresolved, will corrode not just our own culture but all other living cultures.

I've come to this drastic conclusion in light of developments in recent years. We've seen how industrialisation, automation, a booming economy and shorter working hours have given rise to new problems, above all the problem of so-called free time. We're now looking for ways to channel this freedom into cultural activities. Whether or not we'll succeed remains open to question. But there are countries outside Europe that have not yet encountered this problem, that are so far 'behind' in their development that they have not yet found themselves in the fortunate position of having to resolve this problem of structuring free time.

If, as the first step in the application of European methods of design, we could raise the living standards of people outside Europe without diminishing the integrity of their cultures, then I think it would already count as a significant achievement for progressive European thinking.

It is perhaps appropriate to say a word about art here. The trend towards internationalism is undoubtedly also present in art – art as that activity that Hegel described as the expression of man's highest spiritual interests. But the moment art becomes a matter of production, rather than a spiritual exercise, it loses its character as the vehicle for these higher interests. I can scarcely believe that the spiritual needs of Europeans are identical with those of other people who have developed under different conditions. I believe that progressive art needs to be different everywhere, for the very reason that its function – satisfying people's spiritual needs – is everywhere the same.

Art exists to make the improbable real. What arises in an artwork is not a representation of reality as such, but a new reality. Just as reality is different for different people in different places, the new reality represented by the artwork will also vary. And I believe it is precisely in this plurality that we find the essence of what we ought to protect.

responsibility in design and information (1965)

Lecture delivered in English

vision 65 is a congress about communication and information methods, but when will burtin asked me last year in zurich to come i said 'yes', because i had in mind that the subject would be in the field of the shaped environment, that is to say, something close to my own practice and not something so far away as communication and information. but then i thought that visual design – from the spoon to the city – has to do with information and communication, and is also visual communication. and so i came.

it is very hard for me to speak here following the brilliant expositions of the speakers who preceded me. the address given by his excellency, ambassador diop, pointed out so many problems in a right and useful way that it is difficult to add anything. on the other hand the ideas that mr buckminster fuller developed were so much a projection into the future that it is not even possible to discuss them.

in ambassador diop's speech, i appreciated most his approach to the idea of conserving original cultures and understanding the value these original and authentic cultures have for the whole world. this will become even more important in the future, because standardisation on an international level will affect more highly developed civilisations (such as the usa) as well as developing countries (such as the african states).

we all know that we live in a world of accelerating development (the united states is an outstanding example). information and communication are at its basis and are open to great misuse. for what happens? instead of real information and the proper use of the means of communication, we sell gadgets, sell every kind of nonsense, even things nobody needs. this may be one of the reasons why i agreed to come here and to make this point clear, because it is not often enough said.

we live in a world where the smallest problems are not yet very well solved according to human needs; not even the small problems of our environment are solved (which one finds out when one tries to find a good door handle, not to speak of a well-designed city or even part of a city). although we have made enormous technical and scientific progress, our mental and moral progress lags behind, is even in regression. that is to say, the accelerating development of our society is one-sided. properly used means of information and communication are one of the basic conditions for reestablishing balance.

this is the strugle we are now in. with all the scientific methods at our disposal, we have the possibility of proving many things by feeding the problem into a computer. in fact, the computer can be a help for many things. but what does this mean?

in a computer there is an input and there is an output. we have the same system in our brain and also a similar system in our society. when we consider the whole administrative system of a state or of a city, we have a kind of computer with detached programs. however different the input in these administrative systems may be, the output remains more or less the same. the computer is a machine and does what it is told. what counts is the responsibility, in the beginning and in the end, for computerising the data we need to make our society work. in other words, the computer needs direction. the input needs direction, and the output needs direction.

we have, for example, well-working installations for military use. military forces all over the world have very large and interesting machines to figure out possible military scenarios and the actions to take. many of the problems we are confronted with today derive from decisions made by machines, and ultimately by the military people who operate them.

obviously we need another point of view than the military one. but the only thinking machines working on world-size programs today are for military and commercial use. this is the reality we are confronted with. truth has a very weak background. moral and ethical measurements are no longer stable, or are no longer used as they were in older societies. societies must change, of course; all things change. we have the means and methods at hand to get clear information about these problems of changing values. this is the least we can do, and maybe doing so would reestablish a balance of interests.

the future is an open field of possibilities, but we must think over this future, establish something like 'futurology', something like a new science of the future. we can also state our problems to the computer and propose a kind of 'cyberculture'. but the question remains: who is leading this? the consumers certainly are not the leaders. the leaders have to be creative people, people with a certain imagination, people with a certain outlook on the future who are able to take their share of responsibility.

but there is another handicap: computers used in the humanities are often not exact. they are lost if the problem needs interpretation. an interesting example is the story of the computing machine used in a test case for translating a text from english to russian and back to english. when the text came back to english, it was a completely different version from the original, which read 'the spirit is willing but the flesh is weak'. the final translation read 'the ghost is ready but the meat is raw'.

what is apparent in this kind of joke is that somebody must take responsibility for the interpretation, for the choice of medium and for the choice of the final result. who are the people willing and able to do so? i think that these 'leading' people are in the field of design. they must be the designers, not the producers. in the planning field, they must be the planners; in the information field, they must be the informers; in the political field, they must be the politicians. they must be conscious of the need for a very clear response to human needs, both for the individual and for society as a whole. as a matter of consequence, i think that we don't so much need new methods of communication; i sometimes think that even the existing ones are too much, or are misused in such a way that they seem to be too much.

until we learn to use our present resources reasonably and with full responsibility, there is no use for any change. every change brings only more struggle instead of welfare, if the actual problems are not solved. therefore we should find out which mediums are the best ones to give satisfaction to society. and then we must accept responsibility. then we, as architects, publicists, politicians, designers, will be the makers of a world adapted to man in the age of technology.

let me close with a citation about the equality of man from george orwell's *animal farm* and give it a positive instead of a satirical interpretation: 'all animals are equal but some animals are more equal than others'. for us this will mean that the more equal ones – those who know more and have creative minds – have to take on more responsibility. this is a programme in ethics, not one of technical change or so-called progress.

SENSE WITHOUT SENSE? (1965)

As part of this year's Zurich Festival in June the Museum of Applied Arts hosted an exhibition 'Ornament without Ornament?' It opened to a great fanfare. The head of the school of applied arts evidently felt vindicated: the museum and school had gone to a huge amount of trouble, and it had all been worth it. This was the first programmatic exhibition[1] curated by the director of the museum (and director of the school), Mark Buchmann. Years in the making, it was intended to point out new directions, clarify divergent opinions, define a position. The director also made clear his own position when he referred to a prominent colleague as 'also having a passion for ornament'. The exhibition was itself a design project. The striving for ornament in our time, argued Buchmann, was evident in the embossed edge of a paper napkin, in perforated sheet metal, in cast-iron exhaust hoods and the imprints of rubber soles taken from police files. To which we could reply that a paper napkin would fall apart if it didn't have an embossed edge, so its presumed decoration arises from a technical need; that cast-iron exhaust hoods must be profiled in some way, for better adhesion, and the same applies to rubber soles. The curator's passion for ornament therefore produced some notable exaggerations, which were passed off under the banner of 'design'.

DESIGN FOR WHAT?

The ambition of this exhibition is, plainly and simply, to assemble all the arguments in favour of so-called ornament, of little patterns or flourishes of some kind, or other pointless formalisms. That it doesn't wholly succeed is not a consequence of its 'design' but of the perverse nature of its theme.

Much of the installation seems designed to build the case that 'ornament' – as it is defined here – is a major unresolved issue, a means to set the world to rights. And that in a way it is the naughty functionalists who are to blame for the fact that the world is a wasteland, stripped not of things, but of beautiful things. A great number of contributors strive to furnish evidence of this, and compiling this evidence has consumed a great deal of public funds and public sector manhours over a period of two years. The evidence is then spelled out in black and white in a form you can take home and hand down to posterity – a 200-page catalogue with around 300 mostly small-format illustrations. This catalogue, which likewise qualifies as 'design', is divided into five sections and contains much that is shown in the exhibition and then some more, in the form of written contributions. Large segments of the exhibition are unintelligible without these texts; indeed many of the texts read like alibis or apologias.

CLARIFICATION

The title of the exhibition already signals its intentions: it sets out to bemuse, generates confusion, not clarity. Reading the catalogue, one is struck by how the majority of the contributors (bar a few honourable exceptions) flirt with the idea of conferring a new legitimacy on ornament through some back-door route. But at the same time they're always trying to cover their backs: the long period of preparation doesn't seem to have made them any more certain about this undertaking – an undertaking that at most provides a morsel for a discussion, and in no way stretches to an exhibition for public consumption.

A public exhibition, particularly when it's on a hotly disputed theme like this, must be clear, must have a direction, must elucidate concepts rather than obscuring them, must show concrete examples rather than gimmicks.

But what is it, if not a gimmick, to include in such an exhibition photomontages of car headlights and tail-lights? In the best (or worst) case these are decorative, kitsch, impractical, elegant or something along those lines, but they are never ornament. Or what is an Achaemenid ram doing in a section titled 'eulogy'? Is it because someone wanted to present its spiralling horn as ornament, since ornamentation contains spirals now and again? And what about the snake-skins on display in the same location, or the muscle shells, or the filigree carved out of a cigar box by a female poorhouse inmate? And one could go on and on – the exhibition lumps together ornament, decoration, pattern, structure, grid, careful conception and unintended outcome without attempting to distinguish between them or clarify what they are.

MASS PRODUCTION AND PREFABRICATION

It is a fact that the industrialisation of the character of ornament has deprived it of its original significance as a symbol on the one hand, and a decorative impulse, an enhancement of formal quality and expression, on the other. This decline set in early, with the division of labour, serial production and large-scale manufacture. Ornament was estranged from its meaning, becoming a decorative addition. But this role still seems to have some legitimacy, and apart from the much-quoted Adolf Loos ('ornament and crime') and a few who have patently misunderstood him, no one has thought of designating all ornament as superfluous.

But is it really possible to flip the whole thing around, as the 'Ornament without Ornament?' show is now attempting to do? Can everything really be explained in terms of ornament, as with this caption: 'Stackable corrugated cardboard containers. Has the designer not thought of the ornamental effect?' The implication is that the form arises from the stacking of the same object and from this stackability alone! But the form in fact arises out of necessity and is hardly satisfactory from an aesthetic point of view. Or how about the 'legendary Landi-Stuhl'? 'The unassuming hole pattern is strongly determined by the technical aspects of production, although this cannot conceal the fact that its ornamental effect has been taken into account.' The chair is in fact an example of a technical process and a simple hole pattern being united in a form that is consciously not ornamental and senseless. This is clearly not a case of ornament in the standard sense of the term. Another caption is even richer: 'Metal meshwork. The frequent application of this multipurpose "prefabricated" element testifies to its ornamental appeal.' Now there's the rub, the ornamental rub. Meshwork, the most rational way of stretching metal, stiff in one direction, capable of being coiled in another, as the simple, invisible support for plaster walls and ceilings, evidently has 'ornamental appeal'. Here even the innards of walls and ceilings are ornamented!

But what is the point of such budding nonsense? Does it really serve to clarify a problem, and what ultimately is this problem? Is it in fact mass production and prefabrication? Are we talking about ornament made from the stringing together of identical elements? Is this why a facade by Mies van der Rohe is shown, for instance? Because it is a repetition of windows?

IGNORANCE AND INTELLIGENCE

The making of this exhibition involved a whole cohort of collaborators. Some are well-established individuals who are competent in their field. Others are copiers, combiners. Adolf Portmann's text illustrates the confusion surrounding both the terminology and the facts: 'However much such forms may have in common with our ornaments, they are always something other than decoration'. This is said with reference to patterns in the animal kingdom. Or there's Josef Wiedemann's 'the last refuge of ornament is now to be found in design, where it has become cosmetic'.

But what should one make of the lyricist who writes

'the artistic possibilities of non-Euclidean geometry have been overlooked by painters up to now'. Has this man been asleep for the past 30 years, or is he so out of touch that the whole movement passed him by unnoticed? No number of diligent quotations from Hermann Weyl's studies of symmetry will help him if he's really so oblivious to what's going on. Or what basis is there for saying: 'modern design theory since the mid-twentieth century comes down to function: the purpose of the object (its function in the narrower sense) and its constructive principle, which depends on the material (being true to construction) and from the construction (true to materials). The ideal functional object is determined rationally, it is the outcome of a synthesis which its maker has obtained from combining the aspects of structural analysis.' This pitiful twaddle is the kind of thing that is being served up as the definition of 'function'. And you have to wonder what dark springs are being tapped as the putative source of modern design theory and are still, even today, being unhesitatingly invoked against 'function'. In 1948 I gave a lecture titled 'Beauty from Function and as Function' at the Swiss Werkbund's annual conference in Basel. In it I stated among other things, 'It has become clear to us that beauty can no longer be developed out of function alone; instead, the demand for beauty has to be set on the same level as a functional demand, since it is a function too.' In the interim I've offered a host of clarifications of this position, above all in relation to the meaning of the term function, specifically function as a response to people's needs, and the responsibility this places on the designer.

WHAT NOW?

Whether ornament does indeed play the role recently assigned to it by the enthusiasts of applied arts associated with this exhibition, or whether it still on occasion has a worthwhile function, is something that merits careful consideration. But it's plain wrong to take this as the basis for a public exhibition from which every visitor emerges in confusion. It is not good enough to trot out some long-established basic principles with the promise that the seeds of ornament will continue to be nurtured and that the initial project will be spun out with further exhibitions. Because one has to ask: why? And this is the crucial question: why, in heaven's name, was the sleeping dog of ornament woken up and then turned into a monster with a thousand grimaces and a wail that sounds a lot like one of the essential maxims of Alfred Jarry's feral bourgeois King Ubu: 'Isn't a bad law just as valid as a good one?'

1. The exhibition 'Ornament without Ornament?' was shown from June to August 1965 at the Prinz-Carl-Palais in Munich.

DREAMS OF LIFE ON
THE DENTIST'S CHAIR (1964)

In tying the theme of this competition to the year 2000, the aim was to open a window onto developments, both in technology and in the way we live, that are not yet assured, and cannot count as certain.

In the design of our immediate environment, as in many fields, there are things that we cannot yet achieve – not because the technology doesn't exist, but because it hasn't yet been adopted by industry. However it is highly probable, bordering on certain, that industrial applications for these technologies will be found in the foreseeable future. Our technical aspirations for the competition were conceived along these lines, though they were only fulfilled to a small degree. The other aspect of the competition – namely the conceptions of how we'll be living in the year 2000 – produced little that is new. Probably with good reason, for there seem to be no fundamental changes on the horizon apart, perhaps, from a trend towards increasing comfort.

Since it's reasonable to assume that these emerging developments won't be forcibly nipped in the bud, we can draw a series of conclusions about the position of the designer. It is becoming apparent that 'designers' (and I'm using this term fully aware of its meaning) have very little imagination, and only rarely go beyond the everyday – indeed, even then, they're not able to acquit themselves honourably. The activity of the designer, as it is practised, taught and invoked, is not unlike that of the hairdresser, in terms of both the services offered and their impact. For the hairdresser is acknowledged to be useful in his own way, helping to enhance human beauty. A desire to enhance the human environment in the coming decades was the motive behind our competition, or rather the competition that Herr Holzäpfel, with laudable optimism, has brought into being.

I can confirm that the entrants who focused on how we'll be spending our new-found leisure time, a by-product of the reduction in working hours, have largely allowed their imaginations to run riot, producing schemes that belong more in the realm of 'science fiction' or in bad dreams of a life spent in dentist's chairs, ejector seats or rocket ships. (Or in apartments lined with fitted cupboards, none of them a match for the technical or aesthetic clarity of Holzäpfel's Inwand system, which is already enjoying international success.)

… The profession of the designer may be very new, but it has degenerated equally quickly. In the course of a few years, since those hope-filled days, 15 years ago, when we took on the running of the Hochschule für Gestaltung in Ulm, design activity has multiplied. But the only difference between it and the activity of the turn-of the-century draftsman is its new American name. In the meantime, real designers have kept out of the fray and turned to broader interests, namely environmental design as a whole. This situation has given rise to new pedagogical considerations, such as the need to find a way to continue the unbroken but endangered handcraft tradition under the conditions of industrialisation, while ensuring it enjoys the high standing it deserves. For we should not forget that the prospects for an unbroken development in the sector of environmental design depend precisely on the continuity of this handcraft tradition: experience, reason and an openness towards the new possibilities need to rest on a solid foundation of knowledge and skills if we're to achieve the results that we seek – and that we'd really hoped to see in this competition. Still, the experience has confirmed a few points:

1. We are more confident that in the future systematic development will carry more weight than design.

2. The education of designers is inadequate, and in place of the development of manual and intellectual

skills a new academicism, dressed up with a pseudo-terminology, is becoming widespread.

3. In spite of this a few capable people can always find things and form them – things that by virtue of their concept and their form are fully able to fulfil their purpose. These capable people and their creations have been commended here.

RESPONSE TO THE
INTERNATIONAL DESIGN CENTRE
IN BERLIN (1970)

We have created a technology that allows us to do
everything – or rather everything that it is in our power
to imagine. Perhaps not quite yet, but in the near future.
Indeed, with the aid of this technology we'll soon be able
to do things that we can't even conceive of today. By
technology I understand all those aspects of scientific
knowledge that find a real-life application. To indicate just
three principles: increasing speed of communication and
transport; biological manipulation in various guises; the
release of forces that lead to total self-destruction.

The world we live in is apparently unperturbed by
these possibilities. The root-cause for this can be found in
social forms and the way they're governed. Here, rather
than leading to a common understanding, communication
has failed. Nation-states, economic interests and ideologies
are hangovers from atavistic beginnings. Laws, whether
created to limit freedom or protect special liberties, are
obstacles to overcoming outmoded social structures.

Social orders are the frameworks that define the limits
of the world we live in. The extent to which an environment
can be designed depends on the readiness of the social
order not just to permit this activity, but to encourage it.
A humane environment can only arise if the design of the
environment is desired and demanded by society, and
founded on a rational basis. That's still a long way off. But
we mustn't lose sight of this general aim. We must try to
conceive of it as the future, and represent it, demand it. We
know that it won't suddenly and miraculously materialise
before our eyes. We can only edge towards it, bit by bit,

never letting our attention slack. Since this is a long-term goal which cannot be achieved directly, we are moving towards it with small steps. Such small steps can also result in so-called design. In relation to our daily surroundings, our immediate environment, it helps if we can change the small things around us, make them more beautiful, better, cheaper. In this way the life of the individual can become more effective, at work, at leisure, at home, everywhere; more effective, more pleasant and rewarding.

Through this, through the improvement of his own environment, each individual can gain a stronger understanding of the need to improve the environment as a whole. He'll feel a growing need to demand improvements everywhere. And since he, as an individual, is part of society, he will ultimately work towards the common goal of a more humane future. This awareness of the power of personal action has to be strengthened.

There are people to whom such an approach seems naïve and idealistic and who instead prefer to just fool around. Rational, humane thinking is anathema to them. Unwittingly, through their efforts, they are joining the ranks of the profit-anarchists, who likewise think only of themselves, rather than the future of everyone.

I have chosen my path. The path of responsibility and small steps. Broadly speaking, I attempt to influence the political process at a parliamentary level (though this may take too long for some). As a professor of environmental design, the most important thing that I attempt to instil in my listeners is a feeling of responsibility (though this often comes across to them as a romantic design theology). As an architect, I attempt to construct usable objects with the greatest possible functional capacity (though they may not always look particularly spectacular). And as a painter and sculptor, I define certain aesthetic guidelines that can serve as a basis for my aesthetic decisions (though many maintain the outcome of this is not art, which indeed it does not have to be).

Opinions are extremely divided on whether my intentions point the way forwards, or are obsolete. But I am just doing what I can as well as I can. Even if I am not always convinced that it makes sense to try and build a better world for the bad guys, the ignoramuses and the dogmatists, I cannot choose to do anything other than work to the best of my abilities. Ultimately I can console myself with the thought that we have enough good sense to make use of this, if only for the reason that our whole lives – everything we do – can be thought of as a remarkable game that, as history teaches us, does not always turn out to be devoid of meaning or purpose.

FROM FUNCTIONALISM
TO FUNCTION (1979)

It gives me very great pleasure to thank the University of Stuttgart for the honour they have bestowed on me, especially in their 150th year.

I'd like to extend my warm thanks to the rector for the friendly words of his address.

And my admiring thanks also go out to Dean Rittel (Dean of the faculty of architecture and planning), for the way he somehow managed to extract a well-formed encomium out of the outlines of my career, which has run rampant in many different directions.

Finally I'd like to thank the university orchestra for the aesthetic framing of the event, which comes from a time with a more unified culture, it seems, than our own.

My observations will relate to one aspect of this contemporary culture.

Over the past few years a term has come back into use, in a pejorative sense. This term is 'functionalism'. It has to do with the broad field of the design of the environment, with all the objects, large and small, that can be manufactured, seen, used, and their relations to each other.

How has it come about, first, that such objects are now grouped under functionalism and, second, that this designation has acquired pejorative connotations?

It seems necessary to clear up a misunderstanding or rather a sorry misinterpretation here. To begin with, it has to be said that the term 'functionalism' arose at a time when virtually every avant-garde movement was adopting some form of 'ism' as the badge of their progressiveness.

In the broad field of design, functionalism was in ideological competition with constructivism. On the one hand, functionalism emphasised the form that was to be developed out of, or at least justified on the basis of, function. On the other, constructivism emphasised form as the outcome of construction.

Viewed at a remove of more than half a century, the products of that time, for all their different aspirations, seem pretty much alike – though not so much like peas in a pod as eggs of related bird species. As they came to be regarded as the international style, their influence grew and they were – depending on one's ideological standpoint – either decried and fought against, or praised and emulated.

The symbiosis of these two positions, with their multiple levels of interplay, had a particular impact on the appearance of the city, and not just the cities that had to be rebuilt following the war, but also those that had been spared and now found themselves undergoing a process of constant transformation, not to mention the majority of the planned new towns.

The proliferation of 'inhumane' new structures made of concrete, glass, steel and every kind of prefabricated material is increasingly being seen as the legacy of functionalism. Functionalism is coming under attack for this; its twin brother constructivism much less so.

As the development of technical possibilities led to a continual improvement in building techniques, constructivism itself disappeared. It was rightly displaced by construction. Constructivism was never construction; it was a 'simulation' – and ultimately a caricature – of construction.

Moreover a similar thing happened with a parallel development in the so-called liberal arts – the shift from 'simulation', from constructivism towards constructive art. But it is beyond the scope of this talk to pursue how this affects decision-making in aesthetics today.

Functionalism originally arose under the pretext of locating function as either the basis or the justification for design decisions. A primitive example: more light, uniformly larger windows, the glass wall – this represents a perfect concordance between the creative expression of functional-

ism and constructivism and their claim to transparency.
A mutation of functionalism is currently being invoked as
proof of its inhumanity, which is to some extent understandable, but at the same time functionalism generated certain
ways of thinking about function that remain exemplary to
this day.

But what now gives us cause for thought is this:
if functionalism is to blame for some undesirable contemporary developments, it's not for the reasons that have so
far been advanced, but rather because it displayed a lack
of judgement in relation to old, new and altered problems.

Today people rarely think of characterising as 'functionalist' an object that has been developed according to
functional principles. Over time, the difference between a
'simulated functionalism' and the complexity of functions
that determine each designed object has become clear.

What's remarkable and disturbing is that this realisation has changed so little. This is one reason – though
hardly the only one – for the prevailing uncertainty in the
field of design.

Above all, this uncertainty is connected with the fact
that the concept of function seems to be difficult to grasp
in relation to the design of the environment.

If I now put forward my thoughts on this as a contribution to the debate, I do so because I believe, from my
experience, that this will help smooth the way forward.

By function we understand the reciprocal relation
of different factors. In terms of the environment, this means
primarily the relation of people to their surroundings
and the interrelations of environmental factors. There is
no time today to discuss how these factors have to operate
within a socio-economic framework, or which factors are
decisive in this process. But I would like to point out that
environmental factors and interpersonal relations depend
in no small measure on the framework in which they
operate, and that they are always continually influencing
and being influenced by other factors. Yet, taken on its own,
the relation between people and the environment is already
complicated enough.

If one now assumes – as I do – that people have a need for a designed environment that encompasses the arts and the objects of everyday life, then this need has to be approached in the same way as all the other factors that contribute to the making of a meaningful environment. In other words every object, from the smallest to the largest, has to be conceived with a view to achieving harmony not only in its individual functions but also in the way these play against each other. The fact that this goal is inachievable does not absolve us of the responsibility to keep it in our sights as a goal. For even approximate solutions are hard to find when you take all the determining functions into account. Very soon the question arises of the impact of the various solutions on the environment.

If I take seriously this idea of the totality of all functions, then I have also to consider what their repercussions are, in ecological terms, for example, or in relation to energy production or the exploitation of raw materials – in short the whole balance between ecology and economy, on which we are increasingly dependent.

In this context the sheer volume – and quality – of new products that we're daily adding to our environment cannot be a matter of indifference. In the circles that are striving for a higher quality of life and a culture for our time we can hear a widespread call for this to be done in an aesthetically responsible way – though it doesn't yet happen as a matter of course. These calls for a contemporary aesthetic are now closely related to the call for a sparing use of natural resources and the call for an ethical approach to all decision-making.

Thus functionally entwined, ethics and aesthetics are no longer independent from each other; they have practically become synonymous and should be deployed not only retrospectively to assess or critique each new design, but also at the outset of each design process, as the basis for controlling all functions.

Perhaps you think this is just what's going on everyday anyway, that all I'm doing is reheating the daily bread. I'd really like to think this was so. But if I'd been convinced this were the case I would have held my tongue here and simply thanked the university for the honour they've bestowed on me. I'd like to repeat those thanks now and also to thank you, ladies and gentlemen, for your presence and your patience.

THE FUNCTION OF
DESIGNED OBJECTS (1988)

Thirty-five years ago, under the rubric of 'continuity and change', I defined *gestalt* as the harmony of all an object's functions. *Gestalt* is the end-goal of design, but what we have today is design-lite, a fashion phenomenon that has become more or less synonymous with design. Function is no longer 'the harmony of all functions = *gestalt*'; instead, the function of design-lite oscillates between sales promotion and gimmickry. So we find ourselves back where we started, at the point zero that spawned the 'good form' initiative (which held its ground into the 1950s but is now considered outdated). A noxious brand of neo-modernism, running in parallel with a traditional commercial regression into retro-styles, is characteristic of the objects on offer today. Things that are useful, beautifully modest, have become virtually extinct. They have vanished from the market. The simplest utility objects are scarce. At best one can perhaps still hope to buy a decent piece of technical equipment. Designers occupy the role played a century ago by draftsmen, a very different animal. The purpose of the designer has been lost as the economy has boomed, fanning the flames of a throwaway consumer society. Today's situation seems to me pathologically devoid of culture. Civilisation is devouring itself. 'Quality of life' has become a catchphrase. Freedom has given way to the compulsion o consume. The first thing to be noted about the 'function of designed objects', from today's perspective, is that there is now very little interest in this idea. Yet it clearly relates to our whole concept of culture – for designed objects are cultural goods. On top of their utility value, their function is to build the framework in which our culture is expressed. So what do we do, if this framework is diminished?

IMAGE SECTION

Bill with the prototype of his cross-frame chair (Kreuzargenstuhl), Zurich, 1951

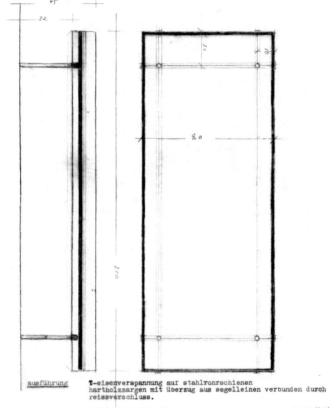

45
32

20
200
80

200

Drawing for a standard bed, produced in a small quantity for Bill's own use, 1931

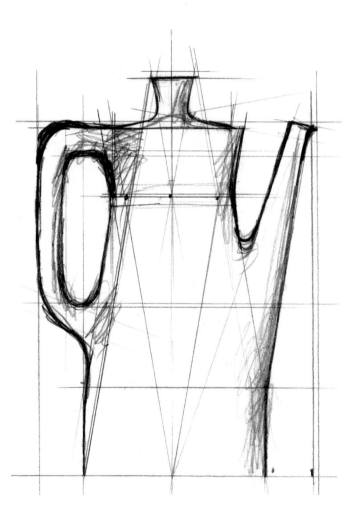

Sketch for a coffee pot in white porcelain for Hutschenreuther, 1956

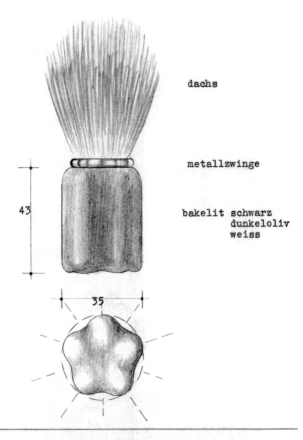

dachs

metallzwinge

bakelit schwarz
       dunkeloliv
       weiss

43

35

INTYP W6	rasierpinsel
	walther a-g oberentfelden
15-1-45	max bill architekt zürich

Design for a shaving brush for Walther, 1945

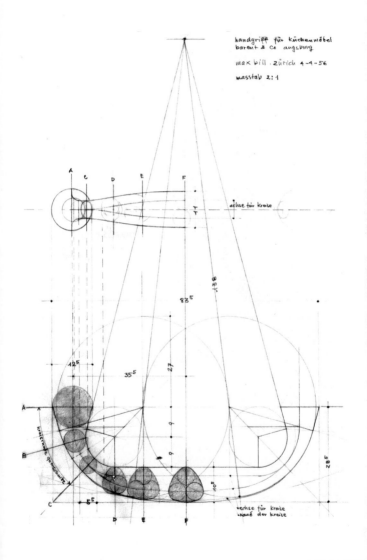

Technical drawing for an aluminium kitchen unit handle, 1956

Prototype of a three-legged chair, 1949

Above: stackable laminated wood chair for Horgen-Glarus, 1950–51
Below: chipboard stool with drawer, a development of the Ulm stool

Above: model of a built-in washbasin for the student housing at Ulm; Below: square-round table with black timber legs for Wohnbedarf/Horgen-Glarus, 1949–50

Prototype of the Rosenthal living sculpture, 1981

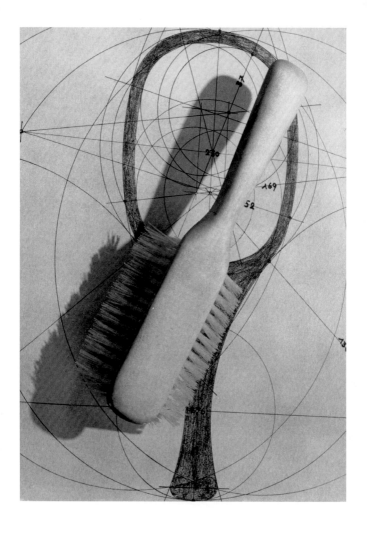

Working drawing for a mirror and model of a hairbrush, 1946

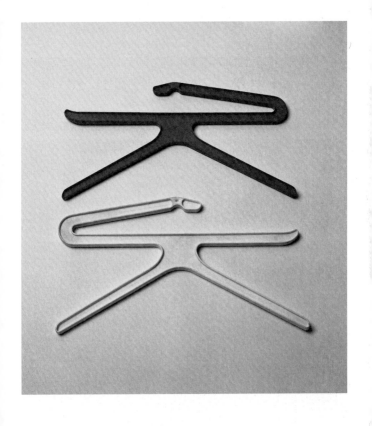

Prototypes of plastic clothes hangers, 1959

Sterling silver flatware, 1955–59

Two designs for wall-hangings, Bill-Salubra, 1957
with the cross-frame chair for Horgen-Glarus, 1951

Architecture Words 5
Form, Function, Beauty = Gestalt
Max Bill

Translated from the German by Pamela Johnston
French translations by Clare Barrett

Series Editor: Brett Steele

AA Managing Editor: Thomas Weaver
AA Publications Editor: Pamela Johnston
AA Art Director: Zak Kyes
Design: Wayne Daly
Series Design: Wayne Daly, Zak Kyes
Editorial Assistant: Clare Barrett

Set in P22 Underground Pro and Palatino

Printed in Belgium by Die Keure

ISBN 978-1-902902-85-2

First published in German by Benteli Verlag, 2008

For a catalogue of AA Publications visit
aaschool.ac.uk/publications
or email publications@aaschool.ac.uk

AA Publications
36 Bedford Square
London WC1B 3ES
T + 44 (0)20 7887 4021
F + 44 (0)20 7414 0783